The Reluctant Rebel

The Reluctant Rebel

A Young Kentuckian's Experiences in the
Confederate Infantry and Cavalry
During the American Civil War

William G. Stevenson

LEONAUR

The Reluctant Rebel: A Young Kentuckian's Experiences in the
Confederate Infantry and Cavalry During the American Civil War
by William G. Stevenson

Originally published under the title:
Thirteen Months in the Rebel Army

Published by Leonaur Ltd

ISBN: 978-1-84677-162-0 (hardcover)
ISBN: 978-1-84677-164-4 (softcover)

http://www.leonaur.com

Publisher's Notes

In the interests of authenticity, the spellings, grammar and place names
used have been retained from the original editions.

The opinions of the authors represent a view of events in which he
was a participant related from his own perspective,
as such the text is relevant as an historical document.

The views expressed in this book are not necessarily
those of the publisher.

Contents

A Word to the Reader

I give to you, in the following pages, a simple narrative of facts. I have no motive to misrepresent or conceal. I have an honest desire to describe faithfully and truly what I saw and heard during thirteen months of enforced service in the Rebel army.

If I should seem to you to speak too favourably of individuals or occurrences in the South, I beg you to consider that I give impressions obtained when in the South. If my book has any value it lies in this very fact, that it gives you an interior view of this stupendous rebellion, which can not be obtained by one standing in the North and looking at it only with Northern eyes.

I have confidence in truth; and unwelcome truth, is none the less truth, and none the less valuable. Sure am I, that if the North had known the whole truth as to the power, the unanimity, and the deadly purpose of the leaders in the rebellion, the government would have been far better prepared for promptly meeting the crisis. Look then candidly at facts, and give them their true weight.

As I am under no obligation, from duty or honour, to conceal what I was compelled to see and hear in the South, I tell it frankly; hoping it may be of value to my bleeding country, I tell it plainly. I have no cause to love the Confederate usurpation, as will fully appear, yet I refrain from abusive and denunciatory epithets, because both my taste and judgment enjoin it.

For the accuracy of names, dates, and places, I rely wholly upon memory. I kept memoranda during my whole service, but was compelled to leave every thing when I attempted escape, as such papers then found in my possession would have secured my certain death; but in all material things I can promise the accuracy which a retentive memory secures.

If an apology is needed for the constant recurrence of the personal pronoun in these pages, let it be said that the recital of personal incidents, without circumlocution, necessarily compels it.

With this brief word, I invite you to enter with me upon the Southern service; you can stop when you please, or go with me to the end, and give a huzza as you see me escape and reach the loyal lines.

William G. Stevenson
New York City
Sept. 15th, 1862

Chapter 1

How I Volunteered

Having spent my boyhood near Louisville, Kentucky, and falling in love with the character of the young men of that chivalric State, I found my way back to that region in the beginning of the year 1861, from my home in the city of New York. In March, I went down the Mississippi river to seek a school, and stopped in Arkansas, where I hoped to find a relative who was engaged in teaching. Failing to find either my kinsman or a remunerative school, I entered into partnership with a young man from Memphis named George Davis, for the purpose of getting out wine-cask staves, to be shipped to New Orleans and from thence to France. We located in Phillips county, Arkansas, bordering on the St. Francis river, more than 100 miles from Memphis. The venture proved profitable, and with five hired hands—Frenchmen—we were making money fast enough to satisfy a moderate ambition, and I had time to look about me and study the various phases of Arkansas society.

Frequent log-rollings—meetings of the neighbours to clear away the dead timber which falls during the winter—brought me into contact with the citizens for miles around. All sought acquaintance with the stranger youth, and were generally courteous and friendly. In trials of strength and skill, I occasionally gained an advantage which made me friends among the older, but evidently waked up envy in the breasts of some of the rougher young men. My refusal to drink with the crowd, also widened the breach which I noticed was forming without any cause on my part.

I was often sounded on the subject of slavery, which is the touchstone always used in the South to test the character of a new-comer. As a young man, I had no very fixed views upon the subject. I had the impression that where it existed it should be left to the control of those who were connected with it; and an outsider, as I was, had better keep hands off, so far at least as any direct efforts were concerned. Nor had I any disposition to promulgate the anti-slavery convictions of my boyhood, since I well knew they could have no good effect there; and as I had met a few radical and half-crazy men in the North, whom I could not avoid opposing, I was able to say some truthful things respecting them, which conciliated my questioners. Yet I would not include the great body of Northerners, whom I admitted I had met in my Kentucky residence (I hailed from Kentucky), as of that hated class called by them "abolitionist;" hence they still looked upon me with a shade of suspicion.

Freedom of opinion in the South upon this subject is not tolerated for a moment, and no honest anti-slavery man was safe for an hour in that section. But as I was only a youth, they were willing to suppose I knew but little of the subject, and I thought that they were satisfied I was not a dangerous resident of their State. While things were in this condition I concluded to write to my parents, who I knew were anxious to hear from me; but I dared not direct a letter to New York, and hence enclosed it in an envelope to a friend near Louisville, Kentucky, with the request that he would "hand it to my father as soon as convenient," not doubting that he would direct and mail it to New York. In this letter, cautiously written, I remarked, "This is a hard place to live in, as I had to ride ten miles to get paper and ink to write this letter;" an unfortunate statement, as will soon appear. The letter was deposited in the post-office on April 16th. I went home, and, as if urged by a guardian, though warlike, spirit, cleaned up my two six-shooters, and, after examining my ammunition, laid them away unloaded. On the night of April 17th, 1861, I was awakened out of a sound sleep about 11 o'clock by three men, who requested me to accompany them to Jeffersonville, a small town on the St. Francis river, eight miles distant. These men I had often met. One of them I regarded as a good friend, and had some confidence in the other two. I asked for time to dress and get ready, which they cheerfully granted. I carefully loaded and capped my "Navies," and saddling my horse started with them, like Paul, "not knowing what was to befall me there," but I fear without much of the spirit of the good apostle, of whom I had learned in the pious home of my childhood. I soon found these "carnal weapons" essential safeguards in that place, though if I had been an apostle I might not have needed them.

On the way to town my friend Buck Scruggs—he deserved a better name—asked me to ride forward with him, and gave me this information and advice. "You are now going to be tried by the Phillips County Vigilance Committee on suspicion of being a Northern man and an abolitionist. When you reach the grocery where they are assembled, seat yourself on the counter in the back part of the room, where if you have to defend yourself they cannot get behind you. Make no studied defence, but calmly meet the charges at the fitting time and in brief words. Keep cool, and use no language which can be tortured into an offensive sense, and if possible I will save you. If the worst comes, draw your pistols and be ready, but don't shoot while ever there is hope, for you will of course be killed the instant you kill any one else."

I listened very intently to this advice, given as coolly as if he had been chatting about an every-day concern, and concluded that all depended upon my coolness and steadiness of nerve when the final struggle came, and resolved to sell my life dearly if it must be sacrificed to the fury of a causeless persecution. To my proposition to escape then, having a fleet horse, he would not assent, as he had pledged his honour to take me to the Vigilance Committee. Honour is as essential among lynchers as among thieves, and all I could do was to brace myself for the encounter, of the nature of which I had but an imperfect conception. About 12 o'clock we reached the place, and I was ushered into the presence of fifty or sixty as graceless scoundrels as even Arkansas can present, who greeted me with hisses, groans, and cries of, "Hang him!" "Burn him!" &c. Two-thirds of the mob were maddened by the vile liquor which abounds in such localities, and few, if any, were entirely sober. The hope that my innocence would protect me, which I had cherished until now, vanished, for I well knew that drunken cut-throats were blind to reason, and rather offended than attracted by innocence.

Order was soon restored, and my friend Mr. Scruggs was called to the chair. In this I saw a ray of hope. The constitution and by-laws of the Vigilance Committee were read; the substance of which was, that in the present troubled state of the country the citizens resolve themselves into a court of justice to examine all Northern men, and that any man of abolition principles shall be hung. The roll was called, and I noticed that a large proportion of the men present were members of the Committee; the others were boatmen and loafers collected about the town. The court of Judge Lynch opened, and I was put upon trial as an "Abolitionist whose business there was to incite an insurrection among the slaves."

The first efforts of the chairman to get the witnesses to the point, were unsuccessful. A mob is not an orderly body, and a drunken mob is hard to manage. General charges were freely made without much point. One cried out, because I refused to drink with them: "This should hang him; he is too white-livered to take a dram with gentlemen, let him swing." "Yes," shouted another; "he is a cursed Yankee teetotaller, hang him." In a quiet way I showed them that this was not the indictment, and that hanging would be a severe punishment for such a sin of omission. To this rejoinder some assented, and the tide seemed for a moment to be setting in my favour, when another urged, "He is too darnd smart for this country. He talks like a Philadelphia lawyer."—Arkansas would be a poor place for the members of the legal profession from the city of brotherly love.—"He comes here to teach us ignorant backwoodsmen. We'll show him a new trick, how to stretch hemp, the cursed Yankee." At length the chairman got them to the specified crime. "An abolitionist! An abolitionist!" they cried with intense rage,—some of them were too drunk to pronounce the word,—but the more sober ones prevailed, and they examined the evidence. The hearsay amounted to nothing, and they plied me with questions as to my views on slavery. I answered promptly, but briefly and honestly, that I held no views on that subject to which they should object, and that I had never interfered with the institution since I came among them, nor did I intend to do so. My calmness seemed to baffle them for a moment, but the bottle was passed, and I noticed that all reason fled from the great majority. Words grew hot and fierce, and eyes flashed fire, while some actually gnashed their teeth in rage. I saw that the mob would soon be uncontrollable unless the chairman brought matters to an end, and suggested, that as there was no evidence against me, they should bring the trial to a close, when to my surprise they produced the letter written to my father but thirty-six hours before, as proof conclusive that I was a Northern abolitionist. I then saw, what I have had abundant evidence of since, that the United States mail was subject to the inspection of Vigilance Committees in the South at their pleasure. The ruffianism of these scoundrels did not allow them even to apologize for their crime. The only phrase in the letter objected to was the unfortunate but truthful one, "This is a hard place." I never felt its force as at that instant. It served as a catch-word for more abuse. "Yes, we'll make it a hard place for you before you get out of it, you infernal spy," &c. The chairman argued rather feebly as I thought—but he understood his audience better than I did—that the letter was free from any proof against me, that I was an innocent-looking youth and had behaved myself correctly, that I evidently did not know much about their peculiar institution, and he thought I had no designs against it. They then went into a private consultation, while I kept my place upon the counter, though gradually moving back to the further edge of it. I saw the crisis was at hand, for smothered but angry argument was going on in knots of men all over the room; my life was suspended upon a breath, and I was utterly powerless to change the decision, whatever it might be; but I must say that my nerves were steady and my hand untrembling,—the unwonted calmness of one who knew that death was inevitable if they should decide in the affirmative on the charge, and who was determined to defend himself to the last, as I well knew any death, they could there inflict, was better than to fall into their hands to be tormented by their hellish hate.

During the consultation, one Butler Cavins, who had a good deal of influence (he owned about twenty slaves), left the grocery with five or six others and was absent about ten minutes. He returned with a coil of rope upon his arm, elbowing his way through the crowd, and exclaimed, "Gentlemen, I am in favour of hanging him. He is a nice, innocent young man. He is far safer for heaven now than when he learns to drink, swear, and be as hardened an old sinner as I am." I could not, even at the peril of life, refrain from retorting: "That, sir, is the only truth I have heard from you to-night." My friends, yet few, and feeble in the advocacy of my cause, seemed slightly encouraged by this rebuff, and gained the ear of the rabble for a little. Cavins could not be silenced. "This is a fine lariat, boys; it has swung two abolitionists. I guess it will hold another. Come on, boys," and a general gathering up in the form of a semicircle, crowding nearer the counter, occurred. At the same moment jumping back off the counter and displaying two six-shooters, I said, "If that's your game, come on; some of you shall go with me to the other world! The first man that makes another step toward me is a dead man." There was one moment of dread suspense and breathless stillness; hands were tightened on daggers and pistols, but no hand was raised. The whole pack stood at bay, convinced that any attempt to take me would send several of them to certain death. My friends, who had kept somewhat to-

15

gether, now ranged themselves against the counter before me, facing the crowd, and Buck Scruggs said, "He has not been convicted, and he shall not be touched." James Niel and Dempsey Jones, the other two who had aided in my arrest, joined Scruggs; and their influence, added to the persuasive eloquence of my pistols, decided the wavering. In twenty seconds, more than twenty votes were given for my acquittal, and the chairman declared in a triumphant voice, "He is unanimously acquitted." The unanimity, I confess, was not such as I would have desired; but all agreed the youngster had pluck, and would soon make as good a fighter as any of them. With a forced laugh, which on some faces ill concealed their hatred, while others made an unseemly attempt at coarse wit, they adjourned, voting themselves a drink at my expense, which I must perforce pay, as they had generously acquitted me! I confess to an amiable wish that the dollar I laid on the counter of Cavins for a gallon of whiskey might some day buy the rope to tighten on his craven throat, though I did not deem it wise to give expression to my sentiments just then.

As the bottle passed for the last time, the change of feeling was most rapid, and I was greeted quite patronizingly by some who had been fierce for hanging me. The more malignant shrunk away by twos and threes, and soon the grocery was empty. My special friends, who were now more than ever friends, having risked their own lives to save me (I even then thought of One who had given up His life to save me), advised, in earnest words—"Now, S., put thirty miles between you and these fellows before tomorrow; for some of them are enraged at their defeat, and if you stay here you are a doomed man."

My first impulse was to return home, attend to my regular business, defy them, and, if necessary, sell my life as dearly as possible. But what could one man, and he a youth and a stranger, do against a corrupt and reckless populace? When suspicion was once aroused, I knew that the least spark would kindle it into a flame. Society there was completely barbarous in its character, so far as law was concerned. The mob has ruled for years, and the spirit of rebellion, now rampant all over the South, had taken form and expressed itself in these vigilance committees, constituting as cruel courts of inquiry as was ever the Inquisition.

Instances of recent occurrence of most atrocious character were in my mind, showing that these men would persecute me to death, sooner or later, if I remained. Only two nights before, a part of this same gang had murdered a Mr. Crawford, who was a native of Sullivan county, New York, but had lived in Arkansas sixteen years—a man against whom no charge could justly be brought. A few days previous to this murder a man named Washburne was whipped to death by four ruffians, of whom Cavins was one. His only crime was that he was a Northern man. His body was thrown into the St. Francis river, after the diabolical deed was consummated. I had heard these horrible recitals until my blood curdled, and I saw there was no hope but in leaving this hell upon earth.

The simple knowledge that I had ever lived in New York would, I think, have hung me without fail that night.

The causes of this mad lawlessness I may not fully understand. Some of them lie upon the surface. Reckless men settled there originally, and, living beyond the control of calmly and justly administered law, they gradually resolved themselves into a court, the most daring and active-minded becoming the self-elected leaders.

Then the system of slavery gives them almost unlimited

power over the persons and lives of large numbers of human beings, and this fosters a spirit of despotism so natural to all men, even the most civilized, when invested with supreme power.

And, still further, some fanatical men from the North, determined violently to break the bonds of the poor slave, had been found in recent years spreading incendiary works among the poor white population and the negroes who could read, thus endangering the lives of the masters and their families. As a matter of self-defence, Northern men were watched with unremitting and eagle-eyed vigilance.

But whether all this explains the fact or not, no Northern man's life was safe for an hour in that section of Arkansas at the time of which I speak. Hence I concluded that their advice was good, though I must lose what interest I had in my business partnership. Then, how was I to travel thirty miles before daybreak, as it was now two o'clock? I immediately took the road to Helena, on the Mississippi river. I will not record all my thoughts during that ride—homeless, friendless, and, though innocent of crime, hunted like a very murderer, in free and enlightened America!

How long is this system of terrorism to continue? This utter disregard of law and the sanctity of human life? Among the questions to be settled by this war, are not these important? Shall an American citizen be allowed in safety to travel or reside anywhere in his own land? Shall there be any freedom of opinion and speech upon the question of slavery?

If it be said that the institution of slavery can not tolerate freedom of thought and speech with safety to the master, then the system is barbarous, and can not exist in a free land. Let it be admitted that there are difficulties connected with the institution; that John Brown raids, and incendiary emissaries, are wicked; that unlicensed denunciations of all implicated in the system, are grossly wrong. Still, can there be no calm and considerate discussion of the rightfulness or sinfulness of the laws which define and regulate slavery? Must all the cruelties and iniquities which accompany its existence be left unchallenged, and their authors uncondemned? Then is the whole system to be swept away as a curse and enormity, which neither the civilization of the nineteenth century nor a just God will longer tolerate?

The blood of hundreds of American citizens, shed on Southern plains with dreadful tortures, cries from the ground, "How long, O Lord, holy and true, dost thou not judge and avenge our blood on them that dwell on the earth?" Has not the day of avenging already commenced?

The intensity of my emotions for three hours had exhausted me, and now the temporary escape from imminent peril allowed me to sink down almost to fainting, scarcely able for a time to keep my seat in the saddle. A feeling of loneliness and utter desertion, such as I have never else experienced, came over me, and I longed once more to be in the free North, and at the home of my affectionate parents.

But as the day broke, I aroused myself to the realities before me, and after procuring breakfast at a private house, rode into Helena, in time to take the Memphis boat, which left at ten o'clock, A.M. This boat, the *St. Francis*, No. 3, left Jeffersonville (where I was tried and released) at seven o'clock in the morning, on its way down the St. Francis river, thence to Helena, and thence up to Memphis. As it left Jeffersonville four hours after my escape from that place, the report that "an abolitionist had been tried that night and ran off," had reached the boat at the wharf. When I took the same boat at Helena at ten o'clock, I heard the excited crowds detailing the incidents in which I had been so deeply interested a few hours before.

It required all the skill in controlling the muscles of my face which I could possibly command, to appear neither too much nor too little interested in what was the theme of every tongue. I was pleased to see that no one thought of the probability of the escaped "abolitionist" having reached that boat, and hence I was not suspected: at least, I thought so. Yet there was nothing in my surroundings that gave me much encouragement, as the passengers, who were numerous, were chiefly violent men and full of denunciation of the North. I was already exhausted by the scenes through which I had passed, and poorly prepared for another and more trying one, which soon met me, and of course was not able to get much rest during the day and night passed on the way to Memphis.

As the *St. Francis* touched the wharf on the morning of the 19th of April, the very day that the blood of the Massachusetts sixth regiment dyed the streets of Baltimore, shed by her murderous rebels, I stepped upon the landing; meaning to look over the state of things in the city, and see if I could get out of it in the direction of Nashville, where I had friends who, I thought, would aid me homeward.

But I had not left the wharf, when a "blue jacket," the sobriquet of the military policemen that then guarded the city, stepped up and said, "I see you are a stranger."

"Yes, sir."

"I have some business with you. You will please walk with me, sir." To my expression of astonishment, which was real, he replied, "You answer the description very well, sir. The Committee of Public Safety wish to see you, come along." As it was useless to parley, I walked with him, and was soon ushered into the presence of that body, a much more intelligent and no less intensely Southern organization, than I had found in the grocery of Jeffersonville.

They questioned me as to my home, political opinions, and destination, and received such answers as I thought it wise to give. Whereupon they confronted me, to my amazement, with a member of the Vigilance Committee which had tried me at Jeffersonville, one hundred and twenty miles distant, thirty hours before. I was amazed, because I did not imagine that any one of their number could have reached Memphis before me. He had ridden after me the night of my escape, and when I stopped for breakfast, he had passed on to Helena, and taking an earlier up-river boat, had reached Memphis some hours in advance of the St. Francis; long enough before me to post the Committee of Public Safety as to my person and story when before his committee. Even with this swift witness against me, they were unable to establish any crime, and after consultation, they told me I could retire. I was immediately followed by the policeman, who handed me a letter written by the chairman, suggesting that I would do well to go directly to a certain recruiting office, where young men were enlisting under the Provisional Government of Tennessee, and where I would find it to my interest to volunteer, adding, substantially, as follows: "Several members of the committee think if you do not see fit to follow this advice, you will probably stretch hemp instead of leaving Memphis; as they can not be responsible for the acts of an infuriate mob, who may hear that you came from the North." I was allowed no time for reflection, as the policeman stood waiting, he said, "to show me the way." I now saw at a glance, that the military power of the city had resolved to compel me to volunteer, and in my friendlessness I could think of no way to escape the cruel and dread necessity.

Still the hope remained that perhaps I might make a partial promise, and ask time, and yet elude the vigilance of the authorities. As the M.P. grew impatient, and at length imperious, showing that he well knew that he had me in his power, I walked on to avoid the crowd which was beginning to gather, and soon reached the recruiting station. I saw, the moment I was inside, that the only door was guarded by bayonets, crossed in the hands of determined men. The Blue Jacket, in a private conversation with the recruiting officer, soon gave him my status; when, turning to me, the officer said, with the air of a man who expects to carry his point, "Well, young man, I learn you have come to volunteer; glad to see you—good company," &c.

To which I replied, "I was advised to call and look at the matter, and will take some time to consider, if you please."

"No need of time, sir—no time to be lost; here is the roll—enter your name, put on the uniform, and then you can pass out," with a glance of his eye at the policeman and the crossed bayonets, which meant plainly enough, "You do not go out before."

To my suggestion that I had a horse on the boat which I must see about, he replied very promptly, "That could all be done when this business was through."

The meshes of their cursed net were around me, and there was no release; and with as good a grace as I could assume, I wrote my name, and thus I volunteered!

Does any reader say, "You did wrong—you had better have died than have given your name to such an infamous and causeless rebellion?" I can only answer: It is far easier to say what a homeless youth, hunted for his life for two nights and a day, until exhausted, faint, and friendless, in the midst of an excited and armed populace, should do, than it was in the circumstances to do what will stand the test of a high, calm, and safe patriotism. Let none condemn until he can lay his hand upon his heart and say, "No conceivable pressure could overcome me."

CHAPTER 2
Infantry Service

The fine horse, which was to have carried me to Nashville and thence to Kentucky, was kindly disposed of by an auctioneer, and the price, minus a handsome commission, handed to me, and then I commenced service in the "Jeff. Davis Invincibles," Co. B, Second Tenn. Volunteers, under command of J. Knox Walker, of Memphis. I still entertained some hope of escape, as I had not yet taken the oath; and I worked hard to obtain information which might aid my purpose. I could find no one to trust, and dare not be too inquisitive about roads and distances.

The first regiment raised in Memphis was composed largely of the upper classes, and represented many millions of property. It was of the same type as the 7th regiment of New York, whereas the second contained about 750 Irishmen, chiefly Catholics, in character like the fine 69th New York. We camped in the Fair Ground, a short distance from the city, an enclosure of some seven acres, surrounded by a high board fence, and guarded by thickly stationed sentinels. As these sentinels were not from our newly-formed regiment, but from trusted companies of older standing, I was soon convinced there was no chance of escape, and resigned myself to the necessities of my lot.

This being once settled, my first resolution was to master all the details of military duty, and perfect myself in drill, feeling conscious of ability soon to rise above the station of a private soldier. This determination saved me from despondency, and was of signal advantage in subsequent adventures.

On May 6th we received orders to proceed to Randolph, sixty-five miles above Memphis, on the Tennessee shore of the Mississippi river, arriving by boat on the 7th. The town of Randolph, which formerly contained about three hundred inhabitants, is situated above high-water mark on a narrow strip of land nearly three hundred yards wide, behind which rises a bluff ninety feet high and very steep. On this bluff, overlooking the town and the river, we established our camp, and here commenced our real soldier's life. The daily routine was as follows: Reveille at 5 A.M.; drill from 5½ to 7½; breakfast, 7½; fatigue call from 8 to 10; orderly call, 10; dinner, 12; fatigue from 1 P.M. to 4; drill and dress parade from 4½ to 7½; supper, 8; tattoo, 9 P.M. The fatigue call did not mean rest, but work.

Thus we toiled for eight weary weeks without rest, except as the Sabbath—the blessed day of rest—gave us some relaxation. My observation, even so early in my military life, convinced me that the observance of the Sabbath is no less a physical necessity than a religious duty—though I can not say that our regiment kept it with a very intelligent view of its sacred character. Our chaplain, Father Daly, celebrated mass in the morning, preached a sermon in the afternoon, and in the evening settled the drunken rows—which were entirely too numerous to recommend to a Protestant youth the religion of which the priest was nevertheless a very favourable representative. His influence was vastly important as a governing power, and he wielded it wisely and kindly.

The idleness of the Sabbath was a great evil, as there was nothing to read, and card-playing and cock-fighting were the chief amusements. This was also our wash-day, and the ration of soap issued for six men was only enough to wash one shirt; hence this was given by lot to one of the mess, and the others were content with the virtue of water alone. While our regiment was often commended for its ability in building fortifications, no one ventured to compliment its cleanliness.

Soon after we camped at Randolph I was appointed third sergeant, and after serving a few days as such was promoted to orderly sergeant. This position, of course, exempted me from actual labour in the trenches, but I had to oversee a squad of workmen. During these two months we, with three other regiments, built Fort Wright, an irregular fortification, inclosing about thirty acres. The fort had no spring of water within the line of entrenchment; and after long deliberation about some means of supplying it with this indispensable article,—during which time we carried every bucket of water used from the river,—the engineers erected a small wheezy second-hand steam-pump on the bank of the river, which was intended to force the water up the bluff into a large cistern that had been constructed for that purpose. The cistern held about a week's supply for two thousand men; but they never seemed to think that a single cannon-ball could smash up the pump and cut off our supply of water. If this defect had been remedied, and the fort had been well armed and manned, it would have been hard to take; but it never availed any thing to the Confederate service. We built four batteries on the bank of the river, three of them mounting three guns each, and the lower one six guns. These guns were 32 and 64 pounders. Three miles further up, above the mouth of Hatchie river, another battery of three 32-pounders was built.

Our rations at this time were neither very lavishly given nor very choice in quality, yet there was no actual suffering. For the first month whiskey was served, and the men were satisfied to work for the promise of forty cents a day extra pay and three drams. In the fifth week the drams were stopped, and the extra pay never began. I am letting that little bill against the Jeff. Davis government, and some larger ones, run at interest. The reader will agree with me that they are likely to run some time.

"Stolen waters are sweet," says high authority, but some of our regiment seemed to set a higher value upon stolen liquor. While the whiskey ration was continued, there was little drunkenness. The men were satisfied with the limited amount given, and the general health of all was good. When the spirit ration was stopped, illicit trade in the "crathur" was carried on by Jews and peddlers, who hung around the camp a short distance out in the woods. The search after these traders by the authorities was so vigilant, that at last there was no whiskey vended nearer than the little town of Covington, eight miles distant. This, however, did not deter the men from making frequent trips to this place after it. Various expedients were resorted to, in order to bring it inside of the guard-lines. Some stopped the tubes on their guns, and filled the barrel with liquor. The colonel, while passing a tent one day, saw one of the men elevate his gun and take a long pull at the muzzle. He called out, "Pat, what have you got in your gun? Whiskey?"

He answered—"Colonel, I was looking into the barrel of my gun to see whether she was clean."

The colonel walked on, muttering something about the curiosity of a man's eyes being located in his mouth. He was no sooner out of sight than Pat inspected his weapon again, and from the sigh of regret which escaped him as he lowered it, I judged that it was "clean dry."

During our stay at Fort Wright, we were all thrown into commotion one day by a mutiny, which for a time threatened very serious consequences. Some of the members of Captain Cosset's company, of our regiment, having found a treasure in the shape of a barrel of whiskey, which an unlucky trader had not concealed securely from their vigilance, got drunk, "*ov coorse,*" and determined to show their independence of military rule by absenting themselves from evening dress-parade. The colonel, noticing the small number present from this company, instructed Lieutenant Beard, then acting captain, to have all the absentees arrested and sent to the guard-house. When parade was dismissed, and the company returned to their quarters, the lieutenant gave the order to one of the sergeants, who was himself intoxicated. On attempting to carry out the order, the sergeant was badly beaten by one of the offenders. A private in the company by the name of Whalen, here interfered and rescued the sergeant from the hands of his assailant. At this moment the regimental quartermaster, Isaac Saffarrens, a brother of the redoubtable hero of Belmont, whose deeds of valour will be duly chronicled, appeared on the scene of action, and attempted to arrest the man Whalen, whose only crime had been committed in saving the sergeant from further beating. Whalen told him that he would not be arrested, as he had not created any disturbance. The quartermaster then tried to seize him, and was knocked down for his trouble. By this time a crowd of officers had hurried to the ground, and the surgeon of the regiment, Dr. Cavenaugh, came to the assistance of his brother officer, and got a pair of damaged eyes for his interference. The drunken company, who were really the proper subjects for punishment, now sided with Whalen, and loaded their guns with the avowed intention of shooting all the officers if they again attempted to take him. In the mêlée that followed, one of the officers shot Whalen, but the ball glanced from his forehead, leaving only a red line on the skin, and he was soon on his feet. He used no weapon but his fist; but he knocked the officers down as fast as they approached. Reinforcements now arrived for the officers. Colonel Walker, seeing that a general mutiny was imminent, ordered out two batteries of light artillery and two companies of infantry. The guns were placed so as to sweep the camp of the mutineers, and they were summoned to surrender. They had entrenched themselves behind a large mass of rock, whence it would have been difficult to dislodge them without serious loss of life. After some deliberation, they agreed to surrender if they were allowed to retain their arms and return to duty. This proposition was of course rejected, and the guns were double-shotted with grape, and a second summons to surrender sent to them. This time they obeyed and threw down their arms, which were secured, and they were soon strongly guarded. I was detailed the same evening, with a number of others, to guard these mutineers. During the night a fight occurred between one of the mutineers and a prisoner in the guard-house. I interfered between them, and was handsomely whipped by both of them. This was too much for any one to stand, and seizing a gun from a sentinel I pinned one of them to the wall of the guard-house with the bayonet, and the other was bound by the guard. I now released the man I had pinned to the wall, and was glad to find that he was only slightly wounded in the side. He was also ironed and confined in the black-hole.

Fourteen of these mutineers were tried in a few days by a general court-martial. Whalen was sentenced to death. Four of the others were sentenced to wear a ball and chain for a month, and lose six months' pay. Three of these being non-commissioned officers were publicly degraded, and put into the ranks. The remainder were sentenced to wear a ball and chain for a month, and lose three months' pay. Whalen's sentence was to have been carried out a month from the time he was tried; but as there was a strong feeling of indignation in the regiment about the severity of his sentence, a recommendation for pardon was presented to General Pillow, and Whalen was reprieved and sent to Memphis. He was at last pardoned, and transferred into a regiment which went to Virginia. This was done that he might not return to the regiment again and encourage others to mutiny, holding out his own example of pardon as a safeguard against punishment.

What effect this leniency had on the future conduct of this regiment will be hereafter seen. It will be observed that this mutiny might have occurred in any army. Others yet to be described had their origin in the defects of the Rebel discipline, and will demonstrate radical evils in their system.

One of the most serio-comic affairs that occurred during my service, may be worth the narration. Shortly after reaching Randolph, one of our sergeants named Brown imported his better-half from Memphis, and for some days they agreed remarkably well; but the sergeant obtaining a jug of whiskey one day, and imbibing too much of the potent fluid, made up his mind that Mrs. Brown should not drink any more, and informed her of his decision. He argued in a masterly way that, as they two were one, he would drink enough for both; and she being fond of the *crathur*, demurred to this proposition. Thereupon ensued a very lively scene. Mrs. Brown, who weighed some fourteen stone, and was fully master of her weight, entrenched herself behind some boxes and barrels, with the precious jug in charge. Mr. Brown first tried compromise, and then flattery, but she was proof against such measures.

Mr. Brown. "Mrs. Brown, my dear, jist come over to me now and we'll argue the matter."

Mrs. Brown. "No, you don't, Sergeant, ye don't catch me wid any ov ye'r compromises. I have the jug now, and I'll hould on to it. So I will."

Mr. B. "Shure, Honey, I was only jokin' wid ye before. Ye may hev half o' the crathur."

Mrs. B. "Now, Sergeant, ye may as well hould ye'r tongue, for a drap ov this liker ye'll never touch agin."

Maddened to desperation, the sergeant attacked Mrs. Brown, who valiantly defended herself with half of a tent-pole which lay near at hand. About this juncture, their "*discussion wid sticks*" was interrupted by the captain ordering out a guard of four men to take the pair and put them in confinement. As I was Orderly Sergeant, I immediately attempted to carry out this order, and arrested the sergeant first. I then advanced to seize Mrs. Brown, but she charged with the tent-pole, and as the four men were engaged in carrying off the sergeant, who resisted desperately, and called lustily to Mrs. Brown for assistance, I was forced to beat a hasty retreat and seek reinforcements, at the same time feeling a very unpleasant tingling sensation across my shoulders from a blow Mrs. Brown had administered with

31

her stick. Being reinforced by several more men, we surrounded the enemy, and she surrendered at discretion, and was put under guard in the middle of the parade ground with her affectionate spouse. Then ensued a scene which almost beggars description.

Mrs. B. O Brown, ye cowardly spalpeen! to stand by and see yer wife abused in sich a manner!

Mr. B. Now, honey, be aisy, can't ye? Shure I was tied before they took ye.

Mrs. B. Shure it was meself that riz ye up out ov the streets, and give ye six hundred dollars that I had in bank, and made a gintleman ov ye; and now ye wouldn't rize yer hand to protect me!

Here Mrs. Brown again became very angry, and would have given her lord a good drubbing, if the guard had not interfered and separated them. Mrs. Brown became so furious that the colonel heard the disturbance, and walked down from his quarters to see what it meant. She immediately demanded to be released, but this the colonel refused; and she then cited many illustrious military men who had been tyrants in some cases, but never so daring as to put a woman under arrest.

Mrs. B. "Now, Colonel, I want to tell ye a thing or two. Gineral Washington, nor the Duke of Willington, nor Napoleon niver put a woman under guard, nor ye haven't any right to do it; and I'll have ye court-martialed, accordin' to the Articles of War. So I will."

Colonel. "Mrs. Brown, if you do not be quiet I will gag you."

Mrs. B. "Ye'll gag me, will ye? Well, I'd like to see ye about it. Ye would make a nice reputation to yerself, gaggin' a woman!"

Colonel. "Very well, Mrs. Brown, I will show you that

I am in earnest. Sergeant, place a gag in that woman's mouth."

Mrs. B. "Och, Colonel dear, ye wouldn't be so bad as that, would ye? Shure, Colonel, I'll be jist as quiet as a lamb. So I will."

Colonel. "Well, Mrs. Brown, if you will promise to behave yourself I will not gag you; but you must not make any more noise."

Mrs. Brown promised obedience and was soon after released, and went to her tent to search for the precious jug and drown her sorrows in another dram; but while the mêlée had been going on I had smashed the jug, and she came back again to bewail her sorrows with Brown, who was still under guard. He was soon after released, and they returned to their quarters a wiser if not a happier pair. That night Mrs. Brown was heard to say:

"Sergeant Brown, ye made a fool ov yerself to-day."

"Yis, Missus Brown, I think we both made a fool of ourself. So I do."

About the first of July we were ordered to Fort Pillow, which is by land fourteen miles above, on the same side of the river. When we reached that place, they were daily expecting an attack from the gunboats, of which we had heard so much, but had not yet seen or feared. Here the commanders wanted to exact the same amount of toil as at Fort Wright; but the men drew up petitions, requesting that the planters, who were at home doing nothing, should send their slaves to work on the fortifications. General Pillow approved of this plan, and published a call for labourers. In less than a month, 7000 able-bodied negro men were at work, and there would have been twice as many, if needed. The planters were, and are yet, in bloody earnest in this rebellion; and my impression, since coming North, is, that the mass of Union-loving people here are asleep, because they do not fully understand the resources and earnestness of the South. There is no such universal and intense earnestness here, as prevails all over the Rebel States. Refined and Christian women, feeling that the Northern armies are invading their homes, cutting off their husbands and brothers, and sweeping away their property, are compelled to take a deeper interest in the struggle than the masses of the North are able to do, removed as they are from the horrors of the battle-scenes, and scarcely yet feeling the first hardship from the war. Indeed, I do not doubt that regiments of women could be raised, if there was any thing they could do in the cause of the South. That they are all wrong, and deeply blinded in warring against rightful authority, makes them none the less, perhaps the more, violent.

The employment of slaves to do the hard work was of great advantage in several respects. It allowed the men to drill and take care of their health, as the planters sent overseers who superintended the negroes. It kept the men in better spirits, and made them more cheerful to endure whatever legitimately belongs to a soldier's life, when they had slaves to do the toilsome work. These slaves were not armed, or relied upon to do any fighting. I have no means of judging how they would have fought, as I never saw them tried.

The natural situation of Fort Pillow is the best I saw on the Mississippi river. It is built on what is called the First Chickasaw Bluff. Fort Wright is on the second, and Memphis on the third bluff of the same name. The river makes a long horseshoe bend here, and the fort is built opposite the lower end of this bend, so that boats are in range for several miles.

The first battery built here was just above high-water mark, and nearly half a mile long. Bomb-proof magazines were placed in the side of the hill; and more than twenty guns of heavy calibre, 32 and 64-pounders, were mounted on double casemate carriages; and it was intended to mount many more. A formidable defence was this expected to be against the gunboats.

We also made a fine military road, thirty feet wide, cut out of the side of the bluff, and ascending gradually to the summit. It served the double purpose of a road, and also a protection for riflemen; as a bank was thrown up on the outer edge of it breast high. Where the road reached the summit of the bluff, was placed a six-inch mortar, mounted on a pivot carriage; and a little further on was a battery, mounting three eight-inch mortars, which were cast in 1804, and looked as if they had seen much service. A great extent of ground was cleared on the summit, and extensive land defences laid out; but while these were in progress we were ordered away.

The river was blockaded a short distance below Fort Pillow in a novel, but not very efficient manner. Flat-boats were anchored in the river about one hundred yards apart, and heavy chain-cables stretched across them. This was intended to stop the boats which should attempt to run past the fort, until the land batteries could sink them. This all did very well, until a rise in the river, when the boats lifted the anchors, broke the chains, floated away down the river, and stuck on a bar several miles below. This blockade was facetiously called by the men, "Pillow's trot-line."

Here again the independent character of the men composing our regiment showed itself more strongly than at Fort Wright. The regiment had now been without pay or bounty for nearly four months, and the men determined to find out why it was not forthcoming. One morning, at drill-call, the men in my own company marched out and stacked their arms, refusing to drill. I then proceeded to call the roll, but no one answered. I then reported to the captain that no one had answered to roll-call, but that all the "absentees were present "in camp. He ordered me to take a guard and arrest every one who refused to fall into ranks. But the question now arose, where was the guard to come from—no one would answer to the guard detail?

The captain went to the colonel, and reported his company in a state of mutiny. Colonel Walker immediately mounted his horse, and galloping to our quarters, ordered the men to take their arms and proceed to the drill-ground. Not a man moved to obey this order, although a few would have done so had they not feared the vengeance of their comrades. The colonel stormed and swore, and assured them that he would have them all shot next morning, if they did not return to duty; but finally, cooling down a little, he demanded of them the reason for refusing to do duty. Some of them answered that they wanted their money. He scornfully asked them, if they came out to fight for the paltry sum of eleven dollars a month; upbraiding them with their lack of patriotism. One of the men remarked, that the officers could afford to be very patriotic, as they drew their pay regularly every month. The colonel then got wrathful again, and ordered out the rest of the regiment to quell the mutiny; but in the mean time they had come to the same resolution, and refused to move. He then placed all the commissioned officers of the regiment under arrest, for not quelling the mutiny. As there was but one other regiment at Fort Pillow at that time, they could not put it down by force. In two days we were paid, and all returned peaceably to duty. Colonel

Walker was then put under arrest by General Pillow, and tried by a court-martial, for allowing his regiment to be off duty for two days, but he was acquitted.

General Pillow, from whom this fort received its name, is a short, stoutly built man, about fifty years of age; has a mild, pleasant expression when not excited; firm, large mouth; grey eyes; hair and whiskers sprinkled with grey. He is fond of the good opinion of his men, and does every thing consistent with military rigor to gain their good-will; nevertheless, he is a strict disciplinarian, and has punished several men with death for desertion and disobedience of orders.

About the middle of August, General Pillow's division, including my regiment, was ordered to Columbus. On our way we passed Island No. 10, which was then being fortified, and did not stop again until we landed at Columbus, Kentucky. This town is situated on the east bank of the Mississippi river, 140 miles above Fort Pillow, and 20 miles below Cairo; while, directly across the river, lie two or three houses which are designated by the name of Belmont.

The hardships of Fort Wright were here renewed; that is, hard work and harder drill. At one time we worked twelve hours out of every thirty-six, so that every other work-turn came at night. Generals Polk, Pillow, Cheatham, and McGown were present day and night, encouraging the men with words of cheer. General Pillow at one time dismounted and worked in the trenches himself, to quiet some dissatisfaction which had arisen. The night was dark and stormy, the men were worn out, and many gave utterance to their dissatisfaction at having to work on such a night. General Pillow was sitting on his horse near by, and occasionally urging on the men the necessity of pressing on with the work; when an old Mexican war veteran, named W. H. Thomas, who was allowed some little latitude by his general called out, "Old Gid, if you think there is so much hurry for this work, suppose you get down and help us a while." The general, seeing that he had an opportunity to gain popularity with the men, dismounted, and laying aside his sword and cloak, worked for several hours. This was a feather in his cap, in the eyes of the poor fellows, for many a day.

An immense amount of work was performed here, and Columbus was often called the "Gibraltar of the Mississippi river," and the Confederate generals fancied that it could not be taken. The town itself is built on a level plain scarcely above high-water mark, as it has been submerged by some of the great floods of former years. A range of hills running parallel to the river, rises directly north of the town. On these hills most of the batteries were erected, and extensive breastworks were also thrown up, since this was the terminus of the Mobile and Ohio railroad, which it was important to keep unobstructed, as the only land communication to Memphis and the interior, should the river navigation be interrupted below Columbus. On the river side were the heaviest batteries. A sand-bag battery mounting six heavy guns, was constructed at the upper end of the town, just in front of General Pillow's headquarters. This battery was constructed by filling corn-sacks with sand, and piling them up in tiers, leaving embrasures for the guns. These tiers were carried several feet above the heads of the men employed in working the guns, so that they were comparatively safe; for if a ball struck the battery, it was merely buried in the sand and no damage done. These guns were thirty-two and sixty-four pounders, brought up from New Orleans. About a mile north of the town, where the bluff juts out flush with the river, a shelf had been formed by a landslide about half way between the level of the river and the summit of the bluff. This shelf was enlarged and levelled, and a battery constructed upon it which completely commanded the river in the direction of Cairo. This battery was large enough to mount ten or twelve heavy guns. On the summit of the bluff was placed a large Whitworth rifled gun, carrying a round shot weighing one hundred and twenty-eight pounds. Minie shot of much heavier weight were also used in this gun. This was one of four which ran the blockade in the Bermuda into Charleston, South Carolina, in the early autumn.

All these works were constructed under the direction of competent engineers, the chief of whom was Captain E.D. Pickett, since adjutant-general to Major-general Hardee.

Torpedoes and other obstructions were placed in the river; but all this kind of work was done secretly by the engineer corps, and the soldiers knew but little of their number and location. Some of these torpedoes were made of cast iron at Memphis and Nashville, and would hold from one to two hundred pounds of powder as a charge. Others were made of boiler iron, of different shapes and sizes. They were to be suspended near the surface of the water by chains and buoys, and discharged by wires stretched near the surface, which a boat would strike in passing over them. I never learned that these infernal machines did any damage, except that one of them nearly destroyed one of their own transport boats, which had incautiously ventured too near its resting-place.

After spending nearly two months in the monotonous camp life of drill and fatigue duty, on the morning of the 7th of November I experienced a new sensation, more startling than agreeable. I had as yet been in no battle, and certainly had no desire to join in a fight against my country and against my kindred, some of whom I had no doubt were in the opposing army, as it was recruited where many of them lived; and I knew they would be loyal to the old flag, and ready to defend it with their lives. But the alarm came so suddenly that I had no time to feign sickness, or invent an excuse for being off duty.

Tappan's Arkansas, and Russell's Tennessee regiments, with a battalion of Mississippi cavalry, about fifteen hundred men in all, who were stationed at Belmont, across the river, were attacked, about seven o'clock, A.M., by General McClernand, with a little over seven thousand men, according to Union authorities. It was a complete surprise to us. At first we thought it was a picket skirmish with the cavalry; but soon Frank Cheatham, our brigadier, came galloping through the camp, bare-headed, in shirt and pantaloons, ordering us to "fall in," saying that the "enemy were murdering the sick men in their tents across the river." The report thus started soon took this form: "The Yankees have bayoneted the sick men in Russell's regiment." This regiment was composed mostly of Irishmen, as was ours. Instantly the rage of our men was such they could scarcely be restrained, and many of them swore they would swim the river if necessary, to reach the enemy, and would give no quarter.

I called the roll of the company, as was my duty, and found seventy-nine men out of one hundred and three present,—there was a good deal of sickness then in the army. Soon four of the company came in from the hospital, declaring they would have a share in the fight; and fourteen who were on guard were added, making the company nearly full.

Two steamboats soon had steam up, and by nine A.M., General Pillow, with his brigade of three thousand five hundred men, was across the river and in the fight.

Up to this time, the Federal force had driven the Confederates back from their camps, and threatened their annihilation, but Pillow's arrival stayed the retreat. By ten A.M., Cheatham's brigade of 2500 men, in which was my regiment, were also coming into the engagement. By eleven A.M., both armies were fully employed. In the mean time some of the guns on the fortifications at Columbus were trying their range upon the Federal gunboats, which lay about three miles distant, and replied fiercely to their challenges. But little execution on either side was done by this firing. The carelessness of the officers in our brigade nearly lost the day, early in the contest. The men had but ten rounds of ammunition, which was soon expended, and we were compelled to retire beneath the bank of the river until more was supplied.

This incident developed a strange, and to me a very sad, trait of human nature,—other illustrations of which I have observed repeatedly since,—an unusual disposition to witticisms in the most solemn circumstances, when it might be supposed that even the most hardened would reflect upon the fearful fate sure to seize upon some of them. One of the captains of our regiment, J.L. Saffarrens, ran into the river waist-deep, in his desire for safety, when one of his men called out, "Captain, dear, are ye off for Memphis? If ye are, tell the ould woman the last ye saw ov me I was fighting, while ye were runnin' away."

The gallant captain received a ball in the face, while stuck in the mud into which he had sunk, and was taken to Memphis with the wounded next day; but I never learned that he delivered the message to the "ould woman." A curious little Irishman in our company, nick-named "Dublin Tricks," who was extremely awkward, and scarcely knew one end of his gun from the other, furnished the occasion of another outburst of laughter, just when the bullets were flying like hail around us. In his haste or ignorance, he did what is often done in the excitement of rapid firing by older soldiers: he rammed down his first cartridge without biting off the end, hence the gun did not go off. He went through the motions, putting in another load and snapping his lock, with the same result, and so on for several minutes. Finally, he thought of a remedy, and sitting down, he patiently picked some priming into the tube. This time the gun and Dublin both went off. He picked himself up slowly, and called out in a serio-comic tone of voice, committing the old Irish bull, "Hould, asy with your laffin', boys; there is sivin more loads in her yit."

Another Hibernian called out to his men, "Illivate your guns a little lower, boys, and ye'll do more execution."

Such jokes were common even amid the horrors of battle. However unseemly, they served to keep up the spirits of the men, to which end other spirits contained in canteens were also freely added. A most reprehensible practice this, for men should go into battle free from unnatural excitement, if they wish to serve the cause in which they are engaged; and moreover, the instances of cruelty which sometimes are perpetrated on the wounded and dying, are caused by the drunkenness of such ruffians as are found in every army.

Our brigade, after receiving ammunition, executed a flank movement on McClernand's left, next the river, while General Pillow was holding their attention in front; this came very near surrounding and capturing the Federal force. For five hours the battle raged with varying success, the Rebel forces on the whole gaining upon the Federals. Our regiment charged and took a part of the 7th Iowa.

A charge is a grand as well as terrible sight, and this one, to my inexperienced eyes, was magnificent. I had often witnessed, with wild delight, the meeting of thunder-clouds in our western storms, the fierce encounter, the blinding lightning, the rolling thunder, the swaying to and fro of the wind-driven and surging masses of angry vapour, the stronger current at length gaining the victory, and sweeping all before it. With an intenser interest and a wilder excitement, did I watch these eight hundred men, as they gathered themselves up for the charge. At the word, every man leaped forward on the full run, yelling as if all the spirits of Tartarus were loosed. In a moment comes the shock, the yells sink into muttered curses, and soon groans are heard, and the bayonet thrusts are quick and bloody. Brute strength and skill often meet, and skill and agility usually win.

The Iowa men were overpowered, and threw down their arms, some four hundred of them, and were sent to the rear, and afterward to Memphis. It was reported that this Iowa regiment had murdered the sick men early in the day, and it was said that some of them were bayoneted after they surrendered. I saw nothing of this, but it may have been so. If so, the author of that accusation was responsible for the barbarity.

I do not doubt such cruelties do sometimes occur in the heat of battle, as there are in all armies some brutal men; but I must do the Rebel officers the justice to state, that they always condemned them, and warned us against acts not sanctioned by the laws of civilized warfare.

The Federals, though fighting well, so far as I know, commenced falling back between two and three P.M. The retreat soon became a rout, and was a running fight to their boats, some three miles. The Confederates pressed them hard, and recaptured several pieces of artillery lost in the early part of the engagement, and did sad execution on the running men; even after they reached the gangplanks of their boats many were shot. I know of no reason why the Union soldiers were routed, unless it was the better fighting of the Rebels. The forces were about equal, and neither had much advantage in ground. General Polk, the commanding general of the Rebels, was not on the ground until near the close of the action, and deserved no credit for the success of his men. General Pillow and Brigadiers Cheatham and McGown, were the efficient commanders that day.

Our wounded, about seven hundred, were carried to the rear during the engagement, and forwarded to Memphis, and we returned and recrossed the river to our camps about seven P.M., completely exhausted. Our company lost, in killed and wounded, twenty-three; the regiment, one hundred and fifteen.

The next day parties were detailed to bury the dead. Ours numbered three hundred. We dug trenches six feet deep and four wide, and laid the bodies in side by side, the members of each company together, the priest saying over them his prayers; the whole closed by three volleys of musketry. The Federal dead were also gathered, and buried in like manner, except the religious services and military salute. Our company buried their dead just before sunset; and when the funeral dirge died away, and the volleys were fired over their graves, many a rugged man, whose heart was steeled by years of hardship and crime, shed tears like a child, for those bound to him by such ties as make all soldiers brothers. One of the worst men in the company excused this seeming weakness to a companion thus: "Tim, I haven't cried this twenty year; but they were all good boys, and my countrymen." The next day when the roll was called, and they answered not, we thought of their ghastly faces as we laid them in the trench, and hearts beat quick. When we sat down to eat and missed a messmate, the query went round, "Will it be my turn next?" A comrade's faults were now forgotten, his good qualities magnified, and all said, "Peace to his ashes."

I may here say, that if one is compelled to fight against his friends, as I was, there are several ways in which he can avoid taking life. A cartridge without a ball, a pretended discharge without a cap, or an extra elevation of the piece, will save his friends and not expose him to suspicion. Not rarely, also, in the heat of battle, a hated officer meets his fate by a ball from his own men, instead of the enemy.

The second day after the battle a sad accident added to the gloom. A crowd had assembled to see the monster Whitworth rifled gun fired off, as it had continued loaded since the day of the fight. She was named the "Lady Polk," and the militant bishop and general was present to add interest to the scene. The gunner warned the crowd that there was some danger, but they heeded not, and pressed close around. The general stood near, why should not others? I stood within thirty feet, and as the gunner ran back with the lanyard, so did I. The next moment occurred the most terrific explosion I had ever heard. As the dust and smoke lifted, we saw the shattered remains of nine men; two more died subsequently from wounds received here. Both the percussion-shell and the gun had burst, and hence the destruction of life. General Polk narrowly escaped; his cloak was swept from him and cut in two as with a sword.

A word of this man, who laid aside his spiritual for military duties, will close my history of soldiering on the Mississippi.

Major-general Leonidas Polk is a tall, well-built man, about fifty-five years of age; hair slightly grey; wears side whiskers, which are as white as snow; aquiline nose, and firm mouth. His voice is a good one for command, and having a West Point education, improved by many years of research on military science, it was expected he would make a skilful general; but the people were much disappointed by his display of generalship in the Western Department, and many clamoured for his removal. It was at one time thought he would be called to the Confederate cabinet as Secretary of State; but this was never done. Many of his old friends and admirers were pained to hear the report circulated, that the good bishop indulged in profanity when he got too deep in his potations; and as these reports were in part confirmed, his reputation suffered greatly.

CHAPTER 3

Ordnance Service

On the 14th of November, I was breveted second lieutenant for the time, that I might take charge of a shipment of ammunition to Camp Beauregard, near Feliciana, a small town in Graves county, Kentucky, near the New Orleans and Ohio railroad, about seventeen miles from Columbus. This place was held by a brigade of about four thousand men, under Brigadier-general John S. Bowen, as a key to the interior, to prevent the Federal forces from attacking Columbus in the rear.

Having now spent six months in the infantry, and mastered the details of a soldier's common duties, I was heartily sick of the life. I sought a transfer to the ordnance department and obtained it, with the rank and pay of ordnance sergeant. Acting on the ever-present purpose, to keep my eyes and ears open and my mouth generally shut, to see and hear all and say little, I knew the ordnance department would open a new field for observation, which might perchance be of use in the future,—a future that was very uncertain to me then, for I could see no daylight as to escape. I may as well admit here, that whenever I reflected on the violation of an oath,—the oath to bear true allegiance to the Confederate Government,—I had some hesitation. An older and wiser head would perhaps have soon settled it, that an oath taken under constraint, and to a rebel and usurped power, was not binding. But I shrunk from the voluntary breaking of even an involuntary bond, in which I had invoked the judgment of God upon me if I should not keep it. To this should be added the consideration, which perhaps had too much weight with me, that as I was trusted by the authorities with a position of some importance, my honour was at stake in fulfilling all my obligations. The idea that I should betray those who were reposing confidence in me at the time and become a deserter, with its odium forever following me, was more than I could contemplate with pleasure. I state this as the exact truth in the case, not as an apology for my conduct. Under this general feeling, I confess I strove more to acquire knowledge where I was, than to escape from the Rebel service.

During the six weeks I was attached to the ordnance department, I learned some facts which it were well for the North to know. Since reaching home, I hear wonder expressed at two things: the vast energy of the South; and their unexpected resources, especially in the procuring of cannon, small-arms, and ammunition. How have they secured and manufactured an adequate supply of these, during such a protracted and destructive struggle?

In answer to this inquiry let me say: The immense supply of cannon—to speak of them first—which that stupendous thief Floyd traitorously placed in the Southern forts and arsenals during his term of office, made a very good beginning for this arm of the service. It was also said by Southern officers, that a large number of guns which had been used in the Mexican war were still stored in the South,—I have heard, at Point Isabel. These were soon brought into use. Many old Mexican and Spanish brass guns were recast into modern field-pieces. These were said to have made the finest guns in the Rebel service, because of the large percentage of silver contained in the metal.

Very early in the rebellion, an extensive establishment for the manufacture of field artillery existed in New Orleans, which sent out beautiful batteries. These batteries I saw in various parts of the army. This factory was under the superintendence of Northern and foreign mechanics. Memphis supplied some thirty-two and sixty-four pounders, also a number of iron Parrott guns. These were cast in the navy yard by the firm of Street & Hungerford. At Nashville, Tennessee, the firm of T.M. Brennan & Co. turned out a large amount of iron light artillery of every description; and shortly before Nashville was evacuated, they perfected a fine machine for rifling cannon, which I examined. They sent a spy North, who obtained, it was said, at the Fort Pitt foundry the drawings and specifications which enabled their workmen to put up this machine. This expensive, and to them valuable machine, was removed to Atlanta, Georgia. In escaping home I came through Nashville a few weeks since, and saw about a dozen large cannon still lying at this foundry, which the sudden flight of the Rebels from Nashville prevented them from rifling or carrying away. All know that the Tredegar Iron Works in Richmond, Virginia, is an extensive manufactory of guns of large calibre. Indeed, every city of the South, having a foundry of any size, boasts of furnishing some cannon.

Many of these guns were defective and even dangerous. One battery from the Memphis foundry lost three guns in a month by bursting, one of them at the battle of Belmont, November 7th. After the Rebel reverses at Forts Henry and Donelson, and the retreat from Bowling Green and Nashville, when General Beauregard took command of the army of the Mississippi valley, he issued a call to the citizens for bells of every description. In some cities every church gave up its bell. Court-houses, factories, public institutions, and plantations, sent on theirs. And the people furnished large quantities of old brass of every description—andirons, candlesticks, gas fixtures, and even door-knobs. I have seen wagon loads of these lying at railroad depots, waiting shipment to the foundries. The Rebels are in earnest.

But the finest cannon have been received from England. Several magnificent guns of the Whitworth and Blakely patents I have seen, or heard described as doing good execution among the "Yankees." How many have been imported I can not tell, but surely a large number. In explanation of my ignorance upon this point, let me state this fact. For some months after the blockade was declared, vessels from Europe were running it constantly, and the Southern papers boastfully told of their success. The Confederate authorities saw the evil of this publicity, and many months ago prohibited the notice of such arrivals. Hence we see no mention of them recently, but it is a great mistake to imagine that there are none. The constant arrival of new European arms and ammunition, the private talk in well-informed circles, the knowledge of the latest European news, and especially the letters from Confederate emissaries regularly received in the South, convince me that the blockade is by no means perfect. From the innumerable inlets all along the south-eastern coast, and the perfect knowledge possessed of these by Rebel pilots, it is perhaps impossible that it should be so. The wisdom of the South in compelling the papers to omit all mention of the facts in this case, is most unquestionable. Well would it be for the North if the press were restrained from publishing a thousand things, which do the readers no good, and which constantly give aid to the Rebel leaders.

As to small-arms, the energies of the South have been more fully developed in their manufacture than is dreamed of by the North. As early as April, 1861, Memphis had commenced the alteration of immense quantities of flint-lock muskets, sent South during Floyd's term as Secretary of War. I saw this work progressing, even before Secession was a completed fact there. New Orleans turned out the best rifles I ever saw in the South. They were similar to the French Minié rifle, furnished with fine sword-bayonets. The Louisiana troops were mostly armed with these. At Nashville and Gallatin, Tennessee, rifles were also made, and I suppose in every considerable city in the South. In addition, it should be known that thousands of Government arms were in the hands of the people, all through the Southern States; how they procured them I do not know. These were gathered up and altered or improved, and issued to the troops. Many of the regiments went into the field armed with every description of guns, from the small-bore squirrel-rifle and double-barrelled shot-gun to the ponderous Brown Bess musket and clumsy but effective German Yager. The regiments were furnished as fast as possible with arms of one kind, and the others returned to the factories to be classified and issued again. Sword-bayonets were fitted to double-barrelled shot-guns, making them a very effective weapon. Others were cut down to a uniform length of about twenty-four inches, and issued to the cavalry. Common hunting-rifles were bored out to carry a Minié ball, twenty to the pound, and sword-bayonets fitted to them. One entire brigade of Tennesseans, under General Wm. H. Carroll, was armed with these guns.

When recovering from sickness at Nashville, I spent hours of investigation in the base of the capitol, used as an armoury, where an immense amount of this work had been done. I have been told that the basement of our National capitol has been used to prepare bread for loyal soldiers; that basement was used to prepare them bullets. At Bowling Green I saw many thousands of rifles and shot-guns which had been collected for alteration, and the machine shop of the Louisville and Nashville railroad was used as an armoury. Many of these guns were destroyed, and others left, when the town was evacuated. Nor should it be forgotten that almost every man of any position owned a pair of Colt's repeaters, many of them of the army and navy size. These were eagerly bought up by the Confederate authorities, who paid from thirty to sixty dollars apiece for them. They were for the cavalry service. Add to these facts, that every country blacksmith made cutlasses from old files, &c.; most of them clumsy but serviceable weapons in a close encounter. Artillery and cavalry sabres were manufactured at New Orleans, Memphis, and Nashville, and probably at other places.

In short, at the beginning of the year 1862, there was rather a surfeit than any scarcity of arms all over the South. Indeed, the energies of the entire people were employed in the production of every description of small-arms, and the enthusiasm displayed rivals the example of ancient Carthage, in her last fruitless struggle against the Romans. And this enthusiasm pervades all classes. I doubt not, if the bow was considered a weapon of war now, the fair maidens of the South would gladly contribute their flowing tresses for bowstrings, if necessary, as did the women of Carthage. Their zeal and self-denial are seen in the fact that the ladies have given vast amounts of jewellery to be sold to build gunboats, fortifications, &c.; the women of Alabama actually contributing $200,000, as estimated, for the construction of a gunboat to protect the Alabama river. Does the reader ask, Why such sacrifice? *They are in earnest.* They think they are fighting for property, home, and life.

Yet after all that has been said, the largest supply of small-arms comes from England and France. I have repeatedly heard it said that 300,000 stand of arms have been received from abroad;—that 65,000 came in one load by the *Bermuda*.

The imported guns are principally Enfield, Minié and Belgian rifles. The first Enfields received had been used somewhat, probably in the Crimean and Indian wars. The crown marks on the first importations, were stamped out with the initials of those who had bought them from the government; the later arrivals, exhibit the crown marks uneffaced. I have seen Enfield rifles of the manufacture of 1861 and 1862, with the stamp of the "Tower" on the lock-plate! Officers, in opening and examining cases of these, would nod significantly to each other, as much as to say, "See the proof of England's neutrality! "The French and Belgian rifles, among the best arms ever made, are mostly of recent manufacture, and elegantly finished. Yes, the South has arms in abundance, and good ones; and they know how to use them, and they are resolved to do it.

The question is often asked, Where does the ammunition come from to supply the Southern army? I would state in reply, that with the cargoes of arms, ammunition was supplied, at the rate of a thousand rounds for each gun. While engaged in the Ordnance Department, I often issued boxes of ammunition, which were put up in London for the Enfield rifle. The fixed ammunition of England is said by Southern officers to be the finest in the world. But much was also made at home. The largest laboratory for making cartridges, of which I had any knowledge, was in Memphis, afterward removed to Grenada, Mississippi. Powder-mills were established at various points, one of the largest at Dahlonega, Georgia; and old saltpetre caves were opened, the government offering forty-five cents per pound for saltpetre, and exempting all persons employed in its manufacture from military duty. Percussion caps were made in Richmond early in 1861, and great numbers were smuggled through the lines, in the early part of the war. As to the supply of ammunition, my opinion is, that the South will not lack while the rebellion lasts.

On the 17th of December, I left Camp Beauregard with a car-load of ammunition, attached to a train of twenty-five box-cars, containing the 27th Tennessee regiment, Colonel Kit Williams commanding, for Bowling Green, where a battle was expected. Colonel Williams' orders were, to go through with all possible dispatch. Here was a new field for observation to me, and one of great interest. As soon as I saw my special charge, the car of ordnance, all right, I doffed my uniform for a fatigue dress, and took my position with the engineer, determined to learn all I could of the management of the locomotive. The knowledge I acquired pretty nearly cost me my life, as will soon be seen,—a new illustration that "a little knowledge is a dangerous thing."

We left Feliciana in the morning, and ran down the New Orleans and Ohio railroad to Union City, 18 miles, thence on the Mobile and Ohio road to Humboldt, which we reached by five o'clock in the evening. It had now grown dusk. During this time, I had mastered the working of the engine, when all was in good order; had noted the amount of steam necessary to run the train, the uses of the various parts of the engine, and had actually had the handling of the locomotive much of the way. When we reached Humboldt, where we took the Memphis and Clarksville railroad for Paris and Bowling Green, the engineer, Charles Little, refused to run the train on during the night, as he was not well acquainted with the road, and thought it dangerous. In addition, the head-light of the locomotive being out of order, and the oil frozen, he could not make it burn, and he could not possibly run without it. Colonel Williams grew angry, probably suspecting him of Union sentiments, and of wishing to delay the train, cursed him rather roundly, and at length told him he should run it under a guard; adding, to the guard already on the engine, "If any accident occurs, shoot the cursed Yankee." Little was a Northern man. Upon the threat thus enforced, the engineer seemed to yield, and prepared to start the train. As if having forgotten an important matter, he said, hastily, "Oh, I must have some oil," and stepping down off the locomotive, walked toward the engine-house. When he was about twenty yards from the cars, the guard thought of their duty, and one of them followed Little, and called upon him to halt; but in a moment he was behind the machine-shop, and off in the dense woods, in the deep darkness. The commotion soon brought the colonel and a crowd, and while they were cursing each other all round, the firemen and most of the brakemen slipped off, and here we were with no means of getting ahead. All this time I had stood on the engine, rather enjoying the mêlée, but taking no part in it, when Colonel Williams, turning to me, said,

"Can not you run the engine?"

I replied, "No, sir."

"You have been on it as we came down."

"Yes, sir, as a matter of curiosity."

"Don't you know how to start and stop her!"

"Yes, that is easy enough; but if any thing should go wrong I could not adjust it."

"No difference, no difference, sir; I must be at Bowling Green to-morrow, and you must put us through."

I looked him in the eye, and said calmly, "Colonel Williams, I can not voluntarily take the responsibility of managing a train with a thousand men aboard, nor will I be forced to do it under a guard who know nothing about an engine, and who would be as likely to shoot me for doing my duty as failing to do it; but if you will find among the men a fireman, send away this guard, and come yourself on the locomotive, I will do the best I can."

And now commenced my apprenticeship to running a Secession railroad train, with a Rebel regiment on board. The engine behaved admirably, and I began to feel quite safe, for she obeyed every command I gave her, as if she acknowledged me her rightful lord.

I could not but be startled at the position in which I was placed, holding in my hand the lives of more than a thousand men, running a train of twenty-five cars over a road I had never seen, running without a head-light, and the road so dark that I could only see a rod or two ahead, and, to crown all, knowing almost nothing of the business. Of course I ran slowly, about ten miles an hour, and never took my hand off the throttle or my eye from the road. The colonel at length grew confident, and almost confidential, and did most of the talking, as I had no time for conversation. When we had run about thirty miles, and every thing was going well, Colonel Williams concluded to walk back, on the top of the box-cars, to a passenger car which was attached to the rear of the train and occupied by the officers.

This somewhat hazardous move he commenced just as we struck a stretch of trestlework which carried the road over a gorge some fifty feet deep. As the locomotive reached the end of the trestlework the grade rose a little, and I could see through, or in, a deep cut which the road ran into, an obstruction. What it was, or how far ahead, I had almost no conception; but quick as thought—and thought is quick as lightning in such circumstances—I whistled for the brakes, shut off the steam, and waited the collision. I would have reversed the engine, but a fear that a reversal of its action would crowd up the cars on the trestlework and throw them into the gorge below, forbade; nor was there wisdom in jumping off, as the steep embankments on either side would prevent escape from the wreck of the cars when the collision came. All this was decided in an instant of time, and I calmly awaited the shock which I saw was unavoidable. Though the speed, which was very moderate before, was considerably diminished in the fifty yards between the obstacle and the head of the train, I saw that we would certainly run into the rear of another train, which was the obstruction I had seen.

The first car struck was loaded with hay and grain. My engine literally split it in two, throwing the hay right and left, and scattering the grain like chaff. The next car, loaded with horses, was in like manner torn to pieces, and the horses piled upon the sides of the road. The third car, loaded with tents and camp equipage, seemed to present greater resistance, as the locomotive only reached it, and came to a stand-still.

My emotions during these moments were most peculiar. I watched the remorseless pressure of the engine with almost admiration. It appeared to be deliberate, and resolute, and insatiable. The shock was not great, the advance seemed very slow; but it ploughed on through car after car with a steady and determined course, which suggested at that critical moment a vast and resistless living agent. When motion ceased, I knew my time of trial was near; for if Colonel Williams had not been thrown from the top of the cars into the gorge below, he would soon be forward to execute his threat,—to shoot me if any accident occurred. I stepped out of the cab on the railing running along to the smoke-stack, so as to be out of view to one coming forward toward the engine, and yet to have him in the full light of the lantern which hung in the cab.

Exactly as I had surmised,—for I had seen a specimen of his fierce temper and recklessness,—he came stamping and cursing; and jumping from the car on to the tender, he drew a pistol, and cried out, "Where is that cursed engineer, that did this pretty job? I'll shoot him the minute I lay eyes on him."

I threw up my six-shooter so that the light of the lantern shone upon it, while he could see me but indistinctly, if at all, and said with deliberation, "Colonel Williams, if you raise your pistol you are a dead man; don't stir, but listen to me. I have done just what any man must have done under the circumstances. I stopped the train as soon as possible, and I'll convince you of it, if you are a reasonable man; but not another word of shooting, or you go down."

"Don't shoot, don't shoot," he cried.

"Put up your pistol and so will I," I replied.

He did so, and came forward, and I explained the impossibility of seeing the train sooner, as I had no headlight, and they had carelessly neglected to leave a light on the rear of the other train. I advised the choleric colonel to go forward and expend his wrath and curses on the conductor of the forward train, that had stopped in such a place, and sent out no signal-man in the rear, nor even left a red light. He acknowledged I was right. I then informed him that I was an officer in the ordnance department, and was in charge of a shipment of ammunition for Bowling Green, and would have him court-martialed when we reached there, unless he apologized for the threats he had made. This information had a calming effect on the colonel, who at heart was really a clever fellow. He afterward came and begged my pardon; we shook hands cordially, and were good friends.

Having settled this talk of shooting, and put the responsibility where it belonged, we had time to look at the damage done by the collision. It was nothing compared with what it might and would have been, if we had been running at high speed. Even as it was, it stirred up the sleeping men not a little. The front train contained a regiment of men, most of whom were asleep, while the employees were repairing an accident to one of the truck-wheels of a car. They had it "jacked up,"' and had all the lights available, including the one from the rear of the train, to aid in their repairs. When we struck them they were driven ahead some thirty feet, and of course their disabled car was still more damaged. Our men were all suddenly waked up, and some of them slightly bruised. The colonel himself was thrown down by the shock, but fortunately did not roll off the car, and was but little injured; and there were no lives lost, except of three of the horses. But we had a toilsome night of it. The debris of the three cars which had been smashed up was carried back through the cut, between the train and the steep sides, and thrown down into the gorge, off the trestlework. The dead horses were drawn up the bank with ropes, and the front train put in running order, after six hours of hard work by as many men as could be employed in such narrow quarters. As the day broke, the forward train moved off; in a few minutes more we followed, and reached Paris by seven o'clock, A.M., December 18, 1861. Thus began and ended my railroad-engineering in Rebeldom. At Paris they found a professional runner, and I resumed my uniform, very thankful to get out of the profession so creditably. Reader, the next time I run a railroad train in such circumstances, may you be there to see it.

On the 19th of December I reached Bowling Green, and found there a larger army than I had before seen,— 65,000 men at least,—under General Albert Sidney Johnson as commander-in-chief, with Generals Buckner, Hardee, Hindman, and Breckenridge on the ground. Floyd came within a few days, bringing about 7000 more. Others were soon added, for on the 25th of December the commissary-general issued 96,000 rations, and by January 1, 1862, 120,000 rations a day. The number of rations shows the whole number attached to the army in every capacity.

During the month of December, sickness in the form of pneumonia and measles became fearfully prevalent, and by the middle of January one-fifth of the army was said to be in the hospital. The prevalence of disease was attributed by the surgeons to the constant rains, the warm winter, and incessant labour day and night on the fortifications.

Though up to this time I had enjoyed uninterrupted good health, the pneumonia now seized me violently; and after a week of "heroic treatment," I was put into a box-car and started for the hospital at Nashville. This was the dreariest ride of my life thus far. Alone, in darkness, suffering excruciating pain, going perhaps to die and be buried in an unhonoured grave, my "Christmas" was any thing but "merry." And yet the month following my arrival in Nashville was the most pleasant, on many accounts, that I had yet spent in Dixie. I was carefully and tenderly nursed by Drs. Stout and Gambling and the ladies of Nashville, who showed the true woman's heart in their assiduous care of the poor suffering men, prostrated by disease and home-sickness. Some of the ladies were strong Secessionists; but I thought then, as I believe now, that most of them, not all, would have shown the same kindness to any suffering soldiers who might have come under their notice. I knew my mother would be a Good Samaritan to a dying Rebel; why should not they to wounded Unionists.

In two weeks I was convalescent, and yet I daily exhausted my returning strength by gaining a knowledge of the Nashville foundries, machine-shops, bridges, capitol, industry, and whatever I thought worth visiting.

At this juncture I also found an old friend of my father's, who with his interesting family did much to make my days of recovery pleasant days; supplying many little things which a soldier's wardrobe and an invalid's appetite needed. How much of a Rebel he was I could never exactly make out, but I think his regard for my family held deep debate with either love or fear of the ruling authorities, to settle the question whether he should aid me to reach home. At least, there was not in what he said in our frequent interviews that entire outspokenness which would have prompted me to make a confidant of him; hence I made no headway toward escaping to the North. Indeed, I considered it the only safe way, in talking with him, to show a guarded zeal for the Southern cause, lest, if he were a hearty Rebel, he might betray me. I am now inclined to the opinion that I was too suspicious of him, and that he was at heart a Union man. At all events, I shall ever be grateful for his kindness to me.

I may as well record at this point what I know of the moral and religious efforts put forth in the South in behalf of the soldiers, and the effect of the Rebellion on the educational and religious interests of the people generally. As a general truth, when the recruits first came to the army, those with religious inclinations or who had pious friends, brought along a Bible or Testament, but these were in most cases soon lost or left behind, and the camps were almost destitute of any good books. Religious publications were not distributed to the soldiers except in the hospitals, and to a very limited extent there. The regiments composed of Irish or French Catholics, usually had a priest as chaplain; but I saw very few of the Protestant chaplains who gave themselves up to the spiritual care of their men. We had a good many ministers in the army of the Mississippi valley, but they almost all held a commission of a military, rather than a religious kind, and so far as I could judge, were fonder of warlike than of heavenly ministrations. In the hospital at Nashville, on the other hand, good men and women endeavoured faithfully to present the truths of the Bible and the consolations of religion to the attention of the inmates. But, as I have hinted, the army was not much benefited by the clerical members attached to it, though their loss may have been felt by the churches they had forsaken. There were but few of what are called Gospel sermons, preached in the army anywhere within my reach during my soldier life. As a consequence of the inherently demoralizing effect of war, and this great destitution of conserving influences, vice reigned almost unrestrained in the army. The few good and devout men, and the infrequent prayer-meetings which were held, seemed powerless to restrain the downward tendency of morals. Profanity, the most revolting and dreadful, abounded, though contrary to the Articles of War, and many of the officers were proficient in this vice. Gambling, in all the forms possible among soldiers, was the main amusement on the Sabbath-day. These were the prominent vices, and, if possible, they were growing more and more monstrous continually.

As for the effect of the war upon the country generally, I can not give many facts, though I had some opportunity of observation, as will be seen. Preaching was maintained in most of the churches in the large cities; but in many of the smaller places, and in country churches, service was suspended. This was true so far as my observation reached, and it must have been so in other places, from the fact that so great a proportion of the men were engaged in the war. And even where preaching was kept up, every sermon I heard was embellished and concluded by a grand flourish, about the duty of praying and fighting for their homes and institutions. This universally belligerent spirit was evidently unfavourable to the progress of true and consistent piety. Schools and seminaries of learning were chiefly closed, and they were not very abundant before. In fine, I think if this Rebellion continues a year or two longer, the South will be a moral wilderness.

CHAPTER 4
Cavalry Service

While at Nashville, recovering from the typhoid pneumonia, I resolved to seek a transfer to the cavalry service, as affording me a new field of observation, and perhaps a more stirring and exciting life. As Captain F——s was recruiting a company in and around Nashville, I rode with him from day to day over the country, and thus secured his advocacy of my wishes. On the 4th of February, 1862, I was transferred to his company, and entered it as orderly sergeant, and a vacancy soon occurring, I was promoted to a lieutenancy, Our company was to have been attached to a battalion commanded by Major Howard of Maryland, formerly of the United States army, and as my captain was in service on General Hardee's staff, I acted as captain during the whole of my term in this branch of the service. Shortly after, my company was attached to the command of that celebrated guerrilla leader, Captain J.H. Morgan, at that time, however, acting under the rules of regular warfare, and not, as now, in the capacity of a highway robber.

The system of guerrilla warfare has been indorsed by an act of the Confederate Congress, and is fully inaugurated over a large part of the South. As there practiced now, it is distinguished from regular warfare by two things: First, the troops are not under any brigade commander, but operate in small bands, much at their pleasure, with a general responsibility to the major-general commanding in their department.

One result of this feature of the system is to develop a large amount of talent in the ranks, as every man has an individual responsibility, and constant opportunities to test his shrewdness and daring. It also gives a perfect knowledge of all roads and localities to the whole force in a given section, as some one or more soldiers will be found in each gang, who, in their frequent maraudings, have traversed every by-path and marked every important point.

The second prominent characteristic of guerrilla warfare, is the license it gives to take by force from supposed enemies or neutrals, horses, cash, munitions of war, and, in short, any thing which can aid the party for which he fights; with the promise of full pay for whatever he brings off to his head-quarters. This is the essential principle of the system, giving it its power and destructiveness. As it displaces patriotism from the breast of the fighter, and substitutes in its room the desire for plunder, the men thus engaged become highway robbers in organized and authorized bands. Nor do guerrilla bands long confine their depredations to known enemies. Wherever a good horse can be found, wherever silver plate is supposed to be secreted, wherever money might be expected, there they concentrate and rob without inquiry as to the character of the owner. Hence the system is destructive to all confidence, and to the safety of even innocent and defenceless females.

It requires no prophet's ken to foresee that the Confederate authorities have commenced a system which will utterly demoralize all engaged in it; destroy the peace, and endanger the safety of non-combatants, and eventually reduce to ruin and anarchy the whole community over which these bands of robbers have their range.

This process has already commenced, and if the loyal troops were withdrawn to-day from all Secessia, and the South allowed its independence, the people would find themselves in the hands of bandits to harass and plunder for months to come, and would have long scores of wrongs to right, which have been inflicted upon neutrals and friends of the Rebellion by its professed soldiers. Should the contest continue for two or three years longer, the South bids fair to lapse into the semi-barbarism of Mexico, or the robber-ruled anarchy of Spain after the Peninsular war. The legitimate tendency of the system is understood by the Southern generals, and some of them resisted its introduction; but the desperation of the whole Southern mind swept away opposition, and they are now embarked on a stormy sea, which will assuredly wreck the craft, if it be not sooner sunk by loyal broadsides.

How the government should treat these free-booters when captured, as some of them have been, is plain, if the usual laws of war are to be followed; they are to be punished as outlaws, and hung or shot. But, in this case, can it be done safely? There were, when I left Secessia, not less than 10,000 men organized as guerrillas. There may be far more at this writing. Is it possible to treat such a number as banditti, without inaugurating a more bloody retaliation and massacre than the world has ever seen? I only raise the question.

Morgan, as a citizen in times of peace, maintained the reputation of a generous, genial, jolly, horse-loving, and horse-racing Kentuckian. He went into the Rebellion *con amore*, and pursues it with high enjoyment. He is about thirty-five years of age, six feet in height, well made for strength and agility, and is perfectly master of himself; has a light complexion, sandy hair, and generally wears a moustache, and a little beard on his chin. His eyes are keen, bluish grey in colour, and when at rest, have a sleepy look, but he sees every one and every thing around him, although apparently unobservant. He is an admirable horseman, and a good shot. As a leader of a battalion of cavalry, he has no superior in the Rebel ranks. His command of his men is supreme. While they admire his generosity and manliness, sharing with them all the hardships of the field, they fear his more than Napoleonic severity for any departure from enjoined duty. His men narrate of him this—that upon one occasion, when engaging in a battle, he directed one of his troopers to perform a hazardous mission in the face of the enemy. The man did not move. Morgan asked, in short quick words,

"Do you understand my orders?"

"Yes, captain, but I can not obey."

"Then, good-by," said Morgan, and in a moment the cavalryman fell dead from his saddle. Turning to his men, he added, "Such be the fate of every man disobeying orders in the face of an enemy."

No man ever hesitated after that to obey any command.

But Morgan is not without generosity to a foe. A Federal cavalryman related to me, since my escape, an unusual act for an enemy. Losing the command of his wounded horse, which goaded by pain plunged wildly on, he was borne into the midst of Morgan's force. "Don't shoot him!" cried Morgan to a dozen of his men who raised their pistols. "Give him a chance for his life." The pistols were lowered and the man sent back to his own lines unharmed. Few men have appeared on either side in this contest who combine dash and caution, intrepidity and calmness, boldness of plan with self-possession in execution, as does Morgan. The feat reported of him in Nashville, shortly after the Rebel army retreated through it, illustrates this. Coming into the city full of Federal soldiers in the garb of a farmer with a load of meal, he generously gives it to the commissary department, saying, in an undertone, that there are some Union men out where he lives, but they have to be careful to dodge the Rebel cavalry, and he wishes to show his love for the cause by this little donation. Going to the St. Cloud to dine, he sits at the same table with General McCook, since cruelly murdered, and is pointed out to the Federal officer as the Union man who had made the generous gift. He is persuaded to take the value of it in gold, and then, in a private interview, tells the Federal officer that a band of Morgan's cavalry is camping near him, and if one or two hundred cavalry will come down there to-morrow he will show them how to take Morgan. The cavalry go, and are taken by Morgan. So the story goes. An equally successful feat it was, to step into the telegraph office in Gallatin, Tennessee, at a later date, as he did, dressed as a Federal officer, and there learn from the operator the time when the down-train would be in, and arrest it, securing many thousands of dollars without loss of men or time. Another anecdote of his cool daring and recklessness is this. Riding up to a picket post near Nashville, dressed in full Federal uniform, he sharply reproved the sentinel on duty for not calling out the guard to salute the officer of the day, as he announced himself to be. The sentinel stammered out, as an excuse, that he did not know him to be the officer of the day. Morgan ordered him to give up his arms, because of this breach of duty, and the man obeyed. He then called out the remaining six men of the guard, including the lieutenant who was in charge, and put them under arrest, ordering them to pile their arms, which they did. He then marched them down the road a short distance where his own men were concealed, and secured all of them, and their arms and horses, without resistance.

In an engagement Morgan is perfectly cool, and yet his face and action are as if surcharged with electricity. He has the quickness of a tiger, and the strength of two ordinary men. One cause of his success is found in the character of his chargers. He has only the fleetest and most enduring horses; and when one fails he soon finds another by hook or by crook. His business in his recent raid into Kentucky (July 28th), seemed to have been mainly to gather up the best blooded horses, in which that State abounds.

Unless in some fortunate hour for the loyal cause he should fall into the hands of the Federal forces, Colonel John H. Morgan will become one of the most potent and dangerous men in the Rebel service.

So far as my observation extended, the Southern cavalry are superior to the loyal, for the kind of service expected of them. They are not relied upon for heavy charges against large bodies of infantry closely massed, as in some of the wars of the Old World during the close of the last century and the first part of this; but for scouting, foraging, and sudden dashes against outposts and unguarded companies of their enemies. In this service, fleetness, perfect docility, and endurance for a few hours or a day, are requisite in the make-up of the horses used. And in these traits Morgan's blooded horses are admirable. And then, with the exception of some of the Western troopers, the Southerners are more perfect horsemen than our loyal cavalry. They have been on horseback, many of them, from youth, and are trained to the perfect control of themselves and their steeds in difficult circumstances. In addition to these causes of superiority, they have a vast advantage over the Federal troops in the present contest from two causes: It is hard to overestimate the advantage they find in a knowledge of the ground, the roads, the ravines, the hiding-places, the marshes, the fords, the forests, &c. But even more important than this is the sympathy they have from the inhabitants, almost universally, who give them information by every method, of the approach, strength, and plans of their enemies. Even the negroes will be found often, either from fear or other motives, to give all the information they can obtain to the Southerners. And the Southerners know far better than we do how to obtain, and sift, and estimate, the value of what the slaves tell them.

From these causes, we should look for and expect no little trouble from the mounted men, who will continue to constitute a pretty large element in the Rebel forces.

After commencing my service in the cavalry, we spent some three weeks in scouting and foraging, having Nashville for our centre. During this time I rode as courier several times, on one occasion riding sixty miles, from Nashville to Shelbyville, in seven hours. Upon another occasion, my blooded horse made fourteen miles in a little less than fifty minutes; but this was harder service than we generally exacted from our horses. Upon reporting myself to General Breckenridge, for whom this arduous service had been performed, he merely said "*Très bien*"—from which I saw that he expected prompt work from those who served him.

On Saturday the 15th of February, the report came that General Johnson would evacuate Bowling Green, and Sunday morning we learned, to the amazement of citizens and soldiers, that Fort Donelson was taken. Never was there greater commotion than Nashville exhibited that Sabbath morning. Churches were closed, Sabbath schools failed to assemble, citizens gathered in groups, consulted hastily, and then rushed to their homes to carry out their plans. Bank directors were speedily in council, and Confederate officials were everywhere engrossed in the plan of evacuation. A general stampede commenced. Specie was sent off to Columbia and Chattanooga, plate was removed, and valuables huddled promiscuously into all kinds of vehicles. Hack-hire rose to twenty-five dollars an hour, and personal service to fabulous prices. Government property was removed as fast as transportation could be furnished. Vast amounts of provisions and ammunition had been accumulated at Nashville, for the armies at Donelson and Bowling Green; and so confident were they of holding those points, that no provision had been made for retreat.

On Sunday the advance of the Bowling Green army began to come in, and those who escaped from Donelson on Tuesday. The appearance of these retreating forces increased the panic among the people, and as the troops came in the non-combatants went out. By the 20th, all who could get away were gone, and none but the military were prominent in the streets, and the sick and wounded were sent southward. The main body of the army camped on the Nashville side of the river. Work was suspended on two fine gunboats in process of construction, and orders given to be ready for their destruction at a moment's notice. The railroad bridge was also prepared for the same fate.

In the mean time the citizens, believing that General Johnson would make a stand, commenced a fortification, four miles from the city, on the south side of the Cumberland, for the purpose of resisting the advance of the gunboats. When it was announced that no defence would be made, the people were highly indignant, because the suddenness of this decision left the citizens no time for the removal of their remaining goods. As the Confederate authorities could not remove all their commissary stores, the warehouses were thrown open, and the poor came and carried off thousands of dollars' worth. Some of these people subsequently set up boarding-houses and fed Union soldiers from the provisions thus obtained.

At length the railroad bridge and the gunboats were burned, and the suspension bridge cut down. An act of pure vandalism was this last, as it neither aided the Rebel retreat nor delayed the Federal advance. Curses against General Floyd and Governor Harris were loud and deep for this act, and General A.S. Johnson never recovered the reputation lost during this retreat.

My company was constantly on scout duty, guarding the roads on the north side of the river, protecting the rear of the retreating hosts, and watching for the coming of Buell's advance. This whole retreat, from Bowling Green to Corinth, a distance of nearly three hundred miles as travelled by the army, and occupying six weeks, was one of the most trying that an army was ever called upon to perform in its own country and among friends. The army was not far from 60,000 strong, after General George B. Crittenden's forces were added to it at Murfreesboro. The season of the year was the worst possible in that latitude. Rain fell, sometimes sleet, four days out of seven. The roads were bad enough at best, but under such a tramping of horses and cutting of wheels as the march produced, soon became horrible. About a hundred regiments were numbered in the army. The full complement of wagons to each regiment—twenty-four—would give above two thousand wagons. Imagine such a train of heavily loaded wagons, passing along a single mud road, accompanied by 55,000 infantry and 5000 horsemen, in the midst of rain and sleet, day after day, camping at night in wet fields or dripping woods, without sufficient food adapted to their wants, and often without any tents, the men lying down in their wet clothes, and rising chilled through and through; and let this continue for six weeks of incessant retreat, and you get a feeble glimpse of what we endured. The army suffered great loss from sickness and some from desertion; some regiments leaving Bowling Green with six or seven hundred men, and reaching Corinth with but half of this number. The towns through which we passed were left full of sick men, and many were sent off to hospitals at some distance from our route.

One of the most desperate marches men were ever called to encounter, was performed by General Breckenridge's division between Fayetteville and Huntsville. They moved at ten A.M., and marched till one o'clock next morning, making thirty miles over a terrible road, amid driving rain and sleet during the whole time. The reason for this desperate work was, that a day's march lay between the rear-guard and the main body of General Johnson's army, and there was danger that it would be cut off. It cost the general hundreds of men. One-fourth of the division dropped out of the ranks unable to proceed, and were taken up by the guard, until every wagon and ambulance was loaded, and then scores were deserted on the road, who straggled in on following days, or made their way back to their homes in Tennessee or Kentucky.

This retreat left a good deal of desolation in its track; for although the officers endeavoured to restrain their men, yet they must have wood; and where the forest was sometimes a mile from the camping ground, and fences were near, the fences suffered; and where sheep and hogs abounded when we came, bones and bristles were more abundant after we left. Horses were needed in the army; and after it left, none were seen on the farms. And then the impressed soldiers, judging from my own feelings, were not over-scrupulous in guarding the property of Rebels. The proud old planters, who had aided in bringing on the rebellion, were unwillingly compelled to bear part of its burdens.

This long and disastrous retreat was rendered a necessity as soon as Fort Henry, on the Tennessee river, was taken by the Federal forces, as this river was opened, and they could throw an army in the rear of the Confederates as far south as Florence, in Alabama, within a few days. Indeed the Confederate officers expected this, and wondered that the Federals failed to do it immediately, as this movement would have cut off Johnson's retreat, and have forced him to surrender, fight, or escape eastward through Knoxville, giving up the whole West to the loyal forces. The delay of the United States forces to take Fort Donelson allowed General A. Sidney Johnson to reach Corinth by March. Here General Beauregard, in command of the army of the Mississippi valley, and already there in person, determined to make a stand.

Great difference of opinion existed among Southern officers as to the expediency of this retreat. Many, among whom were Generals Breckenridge, Hindman, and Bowen, counselled to assume the offensive, and make a bold dash upon Louisville, Ky. This became the general opinion subsequently; and had it been adopted as the policy in the beginning, would have given a different phase to the war in the West, at least for a time.

A ludicrous scene occurred at this time, illustrating the liability to panic to which even brave men are sometimes subject. While resting at Murfreesboro, of course we were liable to be overtaken by Buell's cavalry, and as Colonel Morgan was not a man to be caught asleep, he kept scouting parties ever on the alert, scouring the country on different roads for miles in the direction of the Federal army. I was in command of a squad of eight men, with whom I made a long and rapid march in the direction of Lebanon, and when returning by a different route, night overtook us some fifteen miles from camp. After getting supper at a farm-house, we were again in the saddle at ten o'clock of a calm, quiet evening, with a dim moon to light us back to camp. We jogged on unsuspicious of danger, as we were now on the return from the direction of the Federal cavalry. Within ten miles of camp, near midnight, we passed through a lane and were just entering a forest, when we became aware that a cavalry force was approaching on the same road; but who they were, or how many, we had no idea. We were not expecting another party of our men in this direction, and yet they could hardly be Federals, or we would have heard of them, as we had been near their lines, and among the friends of the Southern cause.

Acting on the principle that it is safer to ask than to answer questions in such circumstances, I instantly ordered them to "Halt," and asked, "Who comes there?" Their commander was equally non-committal, and demanded, "Who comes there?"

"If you are friends, advance and give the countersign," said I; but scarcely was the word uttered when the buck-shot from the shot-guns of the head of the column came whistling past us in dangerous but not fatal proximity. Thus challenged, I instantly ordered, "Draw sabre—Charge!"

and with a wild yell we dashed at them, determined to keep our course toward our camp, whoever they might be. To our surprise, they broke and ran in disorder, and we after them, yelling with all the voice we could command. I soon saw, from their mode of riding and glimpses of their dress, that they were Confederates; but as we had routed them, though seven times our number,—there were sixty-five of them,—we determined to give them a race. Keeping my men together, yelling in unison, and firing in the air occasionally, we pressed them closely six or seven miles. When within three miles of camp, I drew my men up and told them we must get in by another route, and, if possible, as soon as they. A rapid ride by a longer road brought us to the lines in a few minutes, and we found the whole force of over a thousand cavalrymen mounting to repel an attack from a formidable force of Federal cavalry, which had driven in the scouting party of sixty-five men, after a desperate encounter. I immediately reported the whole affair to Morgan, when, with a spice of humour which never forsakes him, he told me to keep quiet; and, calling up the lieutenant who was in charge of the scouting party, ordered him to narrate the whole affair. The lieutenant could not say how many Federal cavalry there were, but there must have been from three to five hundred, from the rattling of sabres and the volume of sound embodied in their unearthly yells. At all events, their charge was terrific, and his wonder was that any of his men escaped. How many of the Federals had fallen it was impossible to estimate, but some were seen to fall, &c.

When Morgan had learned the whole story, with the embellishments, he dismissed the lieutenant. But the story was too good to keep, and by morning the scare and its cause were fully ventilated, greatly to the chagrin of Major

Bennett's battalion, to which the routed men belonged. They were questioned daily about "those three hundred Yankees who made that terrific charge;" and whenever a loud noise of any kind was made, even by a mule, it was asked, with a serious face, if that was equal to "the unearthly yells of the Yankees." Indeed, for weeks, "the three hundred Yankees" was a by-word of ridicule, in reply to any boast from one of Bennett's men.

Before we reached Shelbyville I met with my first wound,—though not from the guns of the Federals. I had chosen a vicious but noble-looking stallion for my Bucephalus, and in rarefying him into submission to Rebel rule, he got the better of me, so far as to land me about a rod over his head, and taking advantage of my being for the moment *hors du combat*, ran over me, struck me with one of his hind feet, and broke my kneepan. But so excited was I with the contest, and smarting under my defeat, that unconscious of the seriousness of my wound, I remounted, and rode four miles to camp at a speed which cooled his ire and taught him some manners. He ever behaved respectably after that, though I always doubted whether he was at heart a true and willing fighter in the Secession ranks, any more than his master. At the end of this race my knee had swollen to twice its usual size, and was exceedingly painful. With difficulty I dismounted, and for days was an invalid, for months lame, and even now at times suffer from the old contusion. Like many another disaster, this proved at length a blessing, as will yet be seen.

The state of society in Tennessee and Alabama, observed on our retreat, calls for no special remarks, except as to its loyalty to the Confederate usurpation. I am often asked respecting the Union feeling in the seceded States, and can only answer, that while I was there I did not see any. My position as an officer was not the most favourable for finding it if it had existed, still I would have seen the smallest evidences had they anywhere cropped out around me, as I was on the lookout for this; and then my last months in the South were spent among the citizens, where I must have seen any Union sentiment if it showed itself at all. The truth is, and it should be stated frankly: the whole people, men, women, and children, were a unit, cemented together under a high heat in opposition to "the invaders."

"But were there not many who if they had opportunity would have proclaimed themselves for the United States Government?" That question is answered in part by the conduct of most of the inhabitants in the Southern cities and neighbourhoods already occupied by the loyal troops. Up to this writing, the developments have not been very encouraging. Yet I doubt not there are some, who in the depth of their hearts believe Secession wrong, and as a principle destructive to all government, and who long for the return of the peaceful and beneficent authority of the Constitution and laws of the Union; but they are too few and timid to exert the smallest influence. Nor dare they attempt it. The tyranny of public opinion is absolute. No young man able to bear arms dares to remain at home; even if the recruiting officers and the conscription law both fail to reach him, he falls under the proscription of the young ladies and must volunteer, as I did, though from not quite the same kind of force. And then, no expression of Union feeling would be tolerated for a moment. From their stand-point, why should it? They feel themselves engaged in a death-struggle, to defend their property, honour, and life. Any hint of Unionism among them is treachery to all their interests, and, besides, a rebuke upon their whole rebellion. When the North becomes as deeply and generally enlisted in the war as the South, and feel it to be a struggle for existence as keenly as they do, no man here will dare to express sentiments favouring the people or institutions of Rebeldom.

"But how," I am asked, "how can good and sensible men, and ministers, even, thus take ground against a beneficent government, and justify themselves in attempting its destruction?" Among the facts I have noted in my brief life, one is this: That the masses of men do not reason, but feel. A few minds give the cue, and the herd follow; and when passion takes possession of the heart, its fumes obscure the brain, and they can not see the truth. A general impression reiterated in a thousand forms, always affirmed and never denied, fills the mind, and is believed to be the truth. And thus it is with the people. "Are they sincere?" Yes, as sincere as ever were martyrs in going to the stake. This is demonstrated by their whole conduct; and conduct is the test of sincerity, while it proves but little as to the righteousness of the cause.

In addition it should be said, the common feeling is, "We are in for a fight, and must carry it through; there is no hope for us but in fighting; if we give up now, our institutions are ruined, and we forever the vassals of the domineering and meddling Yankees." This the leaders and prominent men feel most acutely, and hence they will fight to the last, and keep the people up to that point as long as possible. How long that will be depends upon the will of the North, as no sane man doubts they have the power, and no loyal man questions the right. But the spirit, the enthusiasm, the enlistment of all the people with all their power and resources, are, with the South, as yet far beyond any thing I have seen North.

I may here state that the Confederate authorities have complete control of the press, so that nothing is ever allowed to appear in print which can give information to the North or dishearten their own men. In this it appears to me that they have an unspeakable advantage over the North, with its numberless papers and hundreds of correspondents in the loyal armies. Under such a system it is an absolute impossibility to conceal the movements of the army. With what the correspondents tell and surmise, and what the Confederates find out through spies and informers of various kinds, they are able to see through many of the plans of the Union forces before they are put into execution. No more common remark did I hear than this, as officers were reading the Northern papers: "See what fools these Yankees are. General A—— has left B—— for C——. We will cut him off. Why the Northern generals or the Secretary of War tolerate this freedom of news we can not imagine." Every daily paper I have read since coming North has contained information, either by direct statement or implication, which the enemy can profit by. If we meant to play into the hands of the Rebels, we could hardly do it more successfully than our papers are doing it daily; for it must be remembered that they only need hints and scraps of information, which, added to the antecedent probabilities that our army is about to proceed to a certain point, will enable them to forecast with almost absolute certainty the movements of their enemies. Sure am I, that if a Southern paper would publish such information of their movements, as do the Northern of theirs, the editor's neck would not be safe an hour.

Does any reader aver, "But we see information often quoted from the Southern papers of their movements." Never, until they are made. It is safe to conclude, if you see in a Southern paper any statement that the army is about to do a certain thing, that they will not do any such thing, but something very different. No, the Southern government is now a complete military despotism, and for a successful carrying on of the war against them I think we must adopt, to some extent, the same rigid policy. Freedom of opinion is a precious right, and freedom of the press a valuable boon, but when the publication of news and the utterance of personal opinions endanger the lives of our soldiers, and even the success of our armies, surely it is the duty of the government to restrain that utterance.

Chapter 5
Courier Service

General Breckenridge, about the 1st of April, let me know that he would soon wish me to act on his staff as special aid-de-camp, and advised me to instruct the next officers in command what to do in my absence.

But, before proceeding further, let us return to the movements of the Federal army under General Grant, which we left at Fort Donelson in February.

During the month of March, this army was transported down the Cumberland and up the Tennessee river in boats, and landed at Pittsburgh, near the foot of Muscle Shoals, beyond which large transport boats could not pass. They camped about twenty miles from Corinth, Mississippi, and were awaiting Buell's column, before making an advance on Corinth.

Deserters and scouts gave Beauregard early notice of Grant's flotilla at Pittsburgh Landing, about the 1st of April. Let me here repeat that the Rebel army has an incalculable advantage over the Federal troops, because fighting on their own soil, and where every man, woman, and child is a swift witness against "the invaders."

Beauregard and Johnson in conjoint command, resolved to attack Grant at Pittsburgh Landing before Buell should join him. And here occurred one of those accidents, or providences, as a Christian man rightly regards them, which decided the character of the contest and its result. Grant was expecting Buell with reinforcements; Beauregard was looking for Price and Van Dorn, with 30,000 Missouri and Arkansas troops, who were coming down White River. They were expected to come to Memphis by boat, and to Corinth by rail, and it was hoped they would reach the Rebel forces by Sunday, the 6th of April. Hence our attack was delayed from Saturday the 5th, when we were ready to make it, in order to give time for at least the advance guard of our reinforcements to come up. This delay prevented the complete defeat and rout of Grant's whole force, as the Confederates since believe. I merely give this as their opinion. Indeed, my whole narration of events is intended to present the facts as they appeared to those with whom I was constrained to act. To give as clear a view as possible of the Southern side of that destructive conflict, let the situation and strength of the Rebel army be especially noted. On Thursday, the 3d of April, the preparations for the attack were completed by the commanding generals. Our army then presented a front toward Shiloh cross-roads and church, which place was occupied by General Grant's advance. The right wing, commanded by Brevet Major-general John C. Breckenridge rested at Burnsville, ten miles east of Corinth, on the Memphis and Charleston railroad. The centre and left were massed at and near Corinth, the centre commanded by Major-generals Hardee and Bragg, and the left by Major-general Polk and Brevet Major-general Hindman.

Breckenridge had 11,000 men, Bragg and Hardee about 20,000, Hindman and Polk not far from 10,000. The whole Confederate force was afterward stated in their official reports to be 39,000 men; it probably reached 45,000, but certainly not more. This statement will create surprise, and perhaps denial, but I know whereof I affirm in this. At that time I did not know it, nor did the troops generally have any clear idea of our force.

On Friday the 4th, orders reached us, at two P.M., to prepare five days' rations, roll up our tents, leave them, and be prepared to march in two hours, with forty rounds of ammunition. At the same time an aid from General Breckenridge ordered me to go to his head-quarters, with six reliable men. In a few minutes we answered to the order, every man splendidly mounted, and ready for any mission which he should designate.

With his quick eye he selected one for one duty and one for another, until each had sped away; and turning to me, he said, "You will act as a special aid-de-camp." This announcement I received with especial gratification, as it would relieve me of all actual fighting against the Old Flag, and give me an opportunity to see far more of the progress of the battle which was to ensue than if I were confined to the ranks. The special danger of the mission to which I was called made no impression upon me. I can not recall any time when I had a fear of falling, and I had none then. From that hour until the close of the battle on Monday, I was near General Breckenridge, or conveying dispatches to others from him; hence my narrative of the scenes of the next three days will be mainly of what occurred in General Breckenridge's division, and what I saw while traversing the field of action, which I crossed and recrossed twelve times.

On Friday, at eight P.M., we commenced to move toward Shiloh, in silence, and with great circumspection, the army on different, but converging roads. We made eight miles, and reached Monterey, a little more than seven miles from

Shiloh, at five o'clock on Saturday morning. Here the different divisions formed a junction, and marched forward prepared for action, though not immediately expecting it. We proceeded with extreme caution until within three and a half miles of Grant's pickets, and until our scouts had determined their situation. We could get no nearer without bringing on an engagement; and as General Beauregard had great confidence that the reinforcements would arrive by morning, the afternoon of Saturday was spent in making all necessary disposition of the forces for an early and combined attack on Sunday morning.

While it is no part of my duty, in this narrative, to criticise military movements, and especially those of the Union forces, I may state that the total absence of cavalry pickets from General Grant's army was a matter of perfect amazement to the Rebel officers. There were absolutely none on Grant's left, where General Breckenridge's division was meeting him, so that we were able to come up within hearing of their drums entirely unperceived.

The Southern generals always kept cavalry pickets out for miles, even when no enemy was supposed to be within a day's march of them. The infantry pickets of Grant's forces were not above three-fourths of a mile from his advance camps, and they were too few to make any resistance. With these facts all made known to our head-quarters on Saturday evening, our army was arranged for battle with the certainty of a surprise, and almost the assurance of a victory. Every regiment was carefully and doubly guarded, so that no man might glide away from our ranks and put the Union forces on their guard. This I noted particularly, as I was studying plans of escape that night, that I might put the loyal forces on their guard against the fearful avalanche ready to be hurled upon them. I already saw that they would stand no fair chance for victory, taken completely at unawares. But the orders were imperative to allow no man to leave the ranks, and to shoot the first who should attempt it on any pretence. Then of the nature of the ground between the opposing forces I knew nothing, except that it was said to be crossed and seamed by swamps, in many places almost impassable by daylight, much more so at night. If, then, I should attempt to desert, I must run the gauntlet of our own double guard, risk the chance of making the three or four miles through woods and swamps in deep darkness, and the more hazardous chance, on reaching the Federal lines, of being shot by their pickets. I was therefore compelled to relinquish the hope of escape that night—a sad necessity, for if I had succeeded, it might have saved many Union lives.

About eight o'clock P.M. a council of war was held among the principal generals, and the plan of battle arranged. In an open space, with a dim fire in the midst, and a drum on which to write, you could see grouped around their "little Napoleon," as Beauregard was sometimes fondly called, ten or twelve generals, the flickering light playing over their eager faces, while they listened to his plans and made suggestions as to the conduct of the fight. He soon warmed with his subject, and throwing off his cloak to give free play to his arms, he walked about in the group, gesticulating rapidly, and jerking out his sentences with a strong French accent. All listened attentively, and the dim light just revealing their countenances showed their different emotions of confidence or distrust in his plans. General Sidney Johnson stood apart from the rest, with his tall straight form standing out like a spectre against the dim sky, and the illusion was fully sustained by the light-grey military cloak which he folded around him.

His face was pale, but wore a determined expression, and at times he drew nearer the centre of the ring and said a few words, which were listened to with great attention. It may be he had some foreboding of the fate he was to meet on the morrow, for he did not seem to take much part in the discussion. General Breckenridge lay stretched out on a blanket near the fire, and occasionally sat upright and added a few words of counsel. General Bragg spoke frequently and with earnestness. General Polk sat on a camp-stool at the outside of the circle, and held his head between his hands, seeming buried in thought. Others reclined or sat in various positions. What a grand study for a Rembrandt was this, to see these men, who held the lives of many thousands in their power, planning how best to invoke the angel Azrael to hurl his darts with the breaking of morning light.

For two hours the council lasted, and as it broke up, and the generals were ready to return to their respective commands, I heard General Beauregard say,—raising his hand and pointing in the direction of the Federal camps, whose drums we could plainly hear,—"Gentlemen, we sleep in the enemy's camp to-morrow night."

The Confederate generals had minute information of General Grant's position and numbers. This knowledge was obtained through spies and informers, some of whom had lived in that part of the country and knew every foot of the ground.

Yet that was a dreary night to prepare for the dreadful battle of to-morrow. The men were already weary, hungry, and cold. No fires were allowed, except in holes in the ground, over which the soldiers bent with their blankets round their shoulders, striving to catch and concentrate the little heat that struggled up through the bleak April air.

Many a poor fellow wrote his last sentence in his note-book that night by the dim light of these smothered fires, and sat and talked in undertones of home, wife, and mother, sister or sweetheart. Promises were made to take care of each other, if wounded, or send word home, if slain; keepsakes were looked at again for the last time, and silent prayers were offered by men unused to look above. What an awful thing is war! Here lay, almost within cannon-shot of one another, eighty or ninety thousand men—brothers of the same race and nation, many of them blood relations; thousands of them believing in the same Saviour, and worshiping the same God, their prayers meeting that night at the throne of Heavenly Grace;—yet waiting for the light of the holy Sabbath that they may see how most surely to destroy one another! And yet the masses of these have no ill feeling. It is human butchery, at the bidding of arch-conspirators. Upon them be all the blood shed! A fearful guilt is theirs!

What sleep the men could get on the cold, damp ground, with little protection or fire, they secured during the early part of Saturday night. On Sunday morning, the 6th of April, we were under arms and ready to move by three o'clock.

General Hardee, one of the bravest men in the Confederate service, led the advance and centre, and made the attack. Had I not been called to staff duty, I should have been in the advance with my company. Glad was I that I was not called to fire upon the unsuspecting soldiers of my Northern home. As the day dawned we could hear the musketry, first in dropping shots, then volley after volley, as the battle grew hotter. A little after daylight we passed General Beauregard and staff, who were then over a mile in rear of the troops engaged. He addressed each brigade as it passed, assuring them of a glorious victory, telling them to fight with perfect confidence, as he had 80,000 men available, who should come into action as fast as needed; and wherever reinforcements were wanted, Beauregard would be there. This boast of 80,000 men the officers knew to be false, as he had not a man over 45,000; but as he expected 30,000 under Price and Van Dorn he counted them in, and added 10,000 more to strengthen confidence. But neither he nor any other Confederate general asks any defence for such statements. "Military necessity" will justify any course they choose to take in advancing their cause. After we passed Beauregard, a few minutes of "double quick" brought our division to Grant's advance pickets, who had been surprised and cut down by Hardee's cavalry. This was the first time many of the soldiers had seen men killed in battle, and they stepped carefully around the dead bodies, and seemed to shudder at the sight. General Breckenridge observing it, said quickly, "Never mind this, boys; press on!" Before night, those who remained walked over dead bodies in heaps without a shudder. We soon reached an open field, about eighty rods wide, on the further side of which we could see the camps, and the smoke of battle just beyond. We here made a sharp detour to the right, and ascended a broken range of hills, pressing on for nearly a mile. Here we took position just in front of General Albert Sidney Johnson and staff, and awaited orders. General Breckenridge rode up to General Johnson, and after conversing in a low tone for a few minutes, Johnson said, so that many heard it, "I will lead your brigade into the fight to-day; for I intend to show these Tennesseans and Kentuckians that I am no coward." Poor general! you were not allowed the privilege. We then advanced in line of battle, and General Statham's brigade was engaged first. "Boys," said Breckenridge, "we must take that battery which is shelling Statham. Will you do it?" A wild shout of "Ay, ay, sir," and "Forward to take that battery," was the word; but before we reached the ground it was withdrawn. We now advanced, cautiously, and soon entered the camp of the Seventy-first Ohio Volunteers. By this time, ten o'clock A.M., the battle seemed to be raging along the whole line.

A part of the original plan of battle was to have a space several hundred yards wide between Breckenridge's left and Hardee's right, and thus invite Grant's men into a trap. They refusing to be entrapped, and keeping their front unbroken, Breckenridge sent me to General Johnson for new instructions. When I had come within about ten rods of Johnson's staff, a shell burst in the air about equidistant from myself and the staff. The missiles of death seemed to fill the air in every direction, and almost before the fragments had found their resting-place, I reined up my horse and saluted. General Johnson, who was in front of his staff, had turned away his horse and was leaning a little forward, pressing his right knee against the saddle. In a moment, and before the dispatch was delivered, the staff discovered that their leader was wounded, and hastened to his assistance. A piece of the shell, whose fragments had flown so thick around me as I came up, had struck his thigh half way between his hip and knee, and cut a wide path through, severing the femoral artery. Had he been instantly taken from his horse and a tourniquet applied, he might perhaps have been saved. When reproached by Governor Harris, chief of staff and his brother-in-law, for concealing his wound while his life-blood was ebbing away, he replied, with true nobility of soul, "My life is nothing to the success of this charge; had I exclaimed I was wounded when the troops were passing, it might have created a panic and defeat." In ten minutes after he was lifted from his horse he ceased to breathe. Thus died one of the bravest generals in the Rebel army. My dispatch was taken by Colonel Wickliffe and handed to Harris, who directed me to take it to General Beauregard. When he had read it, he asked—

"Why did you not take this to General Johnson?"

"I did, sir."

"Did he tell you to bring it to me?"

"General Johnson is dead, sir."

"How do you know?"

"I saw him die ten minutes ago?"

"How was he killed?"

I told him. He then dictated two dispatches, one to Governor Harris and one to General Breckenridge, telling them to conceal the death of Johnson, and bidding me not to speak of it to any one. So far as the report of his death was circulated the officers denied it, some affirming that it was Governor Johnson of Kentucky who was killed, others admitting that General A.S. Johnson was slightly wounded. The army knew not of his death till they reached Corinth.

When I returned to General Breckenridge's staff they had advanced half a mile, and were furiously engaged within half-musket range with both small-arms and artillery. About noon General Bowen's brigade—Breckenridge's left—was forced to fall back for ammunition and to reform, their place being supplied by two regiments of Louisiana troops. Here, from two to four P.M., was the hardest fighting in the battle. Breckenridge's own brigade losing nearly one-fourth within two hours. The fire of the Union troops was low and very effective. A battery here did fearful execution among the Rebels with shell, grape, and canister. A wounded gunner belonging to this battery told me the shells were fired with one-second fuses. Our men were ordered to lie down and load, and yet many were killed in this position, so accurate was the fire of the Federal troops. I saw five men killed by the explosion of one shell.

About three o'clock I was sent to the rear with dispatches of the progress of the battle, and asking reinforcements. When about half way to Beauregard's staff, riding at full gallop, my first serious accident occurred, my life being saved by but a hair's breadth. As my horse rose in a long leap, his fore-feet in the air and his head about as high as my shoulder, a cannon-ball struck him above the eye and carried away the upper part of his head. Of course the momentum carried his lifeless body some ten feet ahead, and hurled me some distance further,—sabre, pistols, and all. I gathered myself up, and to my surprise was not hurt in the least. One second later, the ball would have struck me and spared the horse. Thankful for my life, I threw off my sabre and my tight uniform-coat, gave my pistols to a cavalryman near by, and started in search of another horse. General Breckenridge had told me in the morning, if my horse was killed to take the first unemployed one I could find. I knew where some of the infantry field-officers had tied their horses in a ravine in the rear, and while seeking them, I met a scene which lives in my memory as if it were but yesterday.

I had just filled my canteen at a spring, and as I turned from it my eye met the uplifted gaze of a Federal officer, I think a colonel of an Illinois regiment, who was lying desperately wounded, shot through the body and both legs, his dead horse lying on one of his shattered limbs. A cannon-ball had passed through his horse and both of his own knees. He looked pleadingly for a drink, but hesitated to ask it of an enemy, as he supposed me to be. I came up to him, and said, "You seem to be badly wounded, sir; will you have some water?"

"Oh, yes," said he; "but I feared to ask you for it."

"Why?"

"Because I expected no favour of an enemy."

Two other men coming by, I called them to aid in removing the dead horse from his wounded limb. They did so, and then passed on; but I seemed bound to him as by a spell. His manly face and soldierly bearing, when suffering so terribly, charmed me. I changed his position, adjusted his head, arranged his mangled legs in an easy posture, supporting them by leaves stuffed under the blanket on which we had laid him. In the mean time he took out his watch and money, and requested me to hand him his pistols from the saddle-holsters, and urged me to take them, as some one might rob him, and I was the only one who had shown him kindness. I declined, and wrapping them up in a blanket, placed them under his head, telling him the fortunes of war might yet bring his own troops to his side. He seemed overcome, and said, "My friend, why this kindness to an enemy?"

As I gave him another draught of water, I said, "I am not the enemy I seem;" and pressing his hand, I walked quickly on.

He could not live long, but I hope his friends found him as they swept back over the ground the next day.

I soon found a splendid horse, and rode to General Beauregard for orders, and reached my own general about four o'clock P.M. I found that the Federal troops had fallen back more than a mile, but were still fiercely contending for the ground. The Rebels were confident of victory, and pressed them at every point. I had scarce time to mark the condition of things however, until I was again dispatched to the commander-in-chief. I had but fairly started, when I was struck on the right side by a piece of a shell almost spent, which yet came near ending my earthly career. My first feeling after the shock was one of giddiness and blindness, then of partial recovery, then of deathly sickness. I succeeded in getting off rather than falling from my horse, near the root of a tree, where I fainted and lay insensible for nearly an hour. At length, I recovered so far as to be able to remount my horse, whose bridle I had somehow held all the time, though unconsciously. I had ridden but a few rods when a musket-ball passed through the neck of this, my second horse, but, to my surprise, he did not fall immediately. A tremor ran through his frame which I felt, convincing me that he was mortally wounded. I dismounted, and stood watching him. He soon sank on his knees, and then slowly lay down on his side. As his life-blood ebbed away, his eye glazed, and making a last futile effort to rise, he fell back again and died with a groan almost like the last agony of a human being. The pain of my side and my knee, which was never entirely free from pain, grew worse, and I saw that unless I found surgical attendance and rest, I would soon be exhausted. In making my way to the general hospital which was established on the ground where the battle commenced, I met one of Forrest's cavalry, wounded in the foot, and very weak from loss of blood. With my handkerchief and a short stick, I made a simple tourniquet, which stopped the bleeding, when I accompanied him to the hospital. After the dressing of my wound, which was an extensive bruise, about five inches in diameter, I took the cavalryman's horse, and started back to my command. When I had reached the camp of the 71st Ohio Volunteers, my strength failed, and after getting something to eat for myself and horse, and a bucket of water to bathe my side during the night, I tied my horse near the door of a tent, and crept in to try to sleep. But the shells from the gunboats, which made night hideous, the groans of the wounded, and the pleadings of the dying, for a time prevented. Weariness at length overcame me, and sleep followed more refreshing and sound than I hoped for under the circumstances. The sharp rattle of musketry awakened me early, announcing the opening of the second day's battle. But before I speak of Monday the 7th, I will state why the Confederates ceased to fight at half-past five P.M., on Sabbath evening, when they had another hour of daylight. They had already driven back the Federal forces more than three miles along their whole line, had taken 4000 prisoners, including most of General Prentiss's brigade, had captured about seventy pieces of artillery, according to their statement, had taken an immense baggage-train, with vast quantities of commissary, quartermaster's, and medical stores, and had driven Grant's forces under the shelter of their gunboats. Had the battle ended here, the victory would have been most triumphant for the Rebels. Generals Bragg and Breckenridge urged that the battle should go on, that Grant's force was terribly cut up and demoralized, that another hour would take them all prisoners, or drive them into the river, and that then the transport fleet of more than a hundred boats, would be at the control of the Confederates, who could assume the offensive, and in five days take Louisville. Other officers argued that half of their own troops were disabled or scattered, that it would risk the victory already gained to push the remainder of Grant's forces, which now turned at bay, might make a desperate stand. They estimated their own loss at ten or twelve thousand men, and knew that many, thinking the battle was over, had left their commands and were loading themselves with plunder, from the pockets of the dead and the knapsacks lying over the field or found in the Federal camps. Some expressed strong confidence that Price and Van Dorn would arrive during the night, and the victory would be easily completed on the morrow.

While this argument lasted, the men were resting, the hour passed away, and night spread her sable pall over the scene.

The night was spent in removing the wounded, and as much of the captured stores and artillery as possible; but horses and wagons were scarce, and most of the stores and some wounded were left. The Confederates carried off thirty-six pieces of artillery, which were not retaken. Hospitals were established on the road leading to Corinth, and most of the wounded of the first day received every attention possible under the circumstances; though the advance had been made so suddenly, that insufficient attention had been given to providing medical stores and surgical instruments. The scattered regiments were gathered, reorganized, and put, as far as possible, in order for battle, and Beauregard ordered a large cavalry force to stretch themselves out in a line a short distance in rear of the army, to turn back all stragglers, and gave them instructions to shoot any unwounded man retreating. This was rigidly enforced, and some who attempted to escape were shot. Orders were issued to shoot any one found plundering the dead or wounded. Stragglers were forced into the nearest regiment, and every thing done that could be to insure success.

From the foregoing account it will be seen that the following telegram, sent by Beauregard to Richmond, is not far from literally true:

Battle-field of Shiloh
Via Corinth and Chattanooga
April 6, 1862

General S. Cooper, Adjutant-general

—We have this morning attacked the enemy in strong position in front of Pittsburgh, and after a severe battle of ten hours, thanks to Almighty God, gained a complete victory, driving the enemy from every position.

The loss on both sides is heavy, including our commander-in-chief, General Albert Sidney Johnson, who fell gallantly leading his troops into the thickest of the fight.

G. T. Beauregard
General commanding.

The morning of Monday, April 7th, was dark and gloomy; the men were weary and stiffened by the exertions of the previous day, and from the chilling effects of the rain which fell during the night. The dead of both armies lay strewed over the field by hundreds, and many of the desperately wounded were still groaning out their lives in fearful agony. At five A.M. I was in the saddle, though, scarcely able to mount, from the pain in knee and side; and in making my way to General Beauregard's staff, my head reeled and my heart grew sick at the scenes through which I passed. I record but one. In crossing a small ravine, my horse hesitated to step over the stream, and I glanced down to detect the cause. The slight rain during the night had washed the leaves out of a narrow channel down the gully some six inches wide, leaving the hard clay exposed. Down this pathway ran sluggishly a band of blood nearly an inch thick, filling the channel. For a minute I looked and reflected, how many human lives are flowing past me, and who shall account for such butchery! Striking my rowels into the horse to escape from the horrible sight, he plunged his foot into the stream of blood, and threw the already thickening mass in ropy folds upon the dead leaves on the bank! The only relief to my feelings was the reflection that I had not shed one drop of that blood.

I took my position on General B.'s staff at six o'clock in the morning, and remained near him most of the day. The Federal forces had already commenced the attack, and the tide of battle soon turned. Grant's reinforcements had come up during the night, but Beauregard's had not, and early in the day it became evident that we were fighting against fearful odds. Beauregard sent forward 3000 of his best troops, held as a reserve during the first day. They did all that so small a number could do, but it was of no avail. Step by step they drove us back, while every foot of ground was yielded only after a determined resistance. The battle raged mainly on our left, General Breckenridge's division doing but little fighting this day, compared with the first day. General Grant seemed determined to outflank our left, and occupy the road behind us, and as the Confederates had not men enough to hold the camps they had taken, and check this flank movement, retreat became necessary. About nine A.M. I rode to General Beauregard for orders; when returning, I heard the report that General Buell had been killed and his body taken toward Corinth. This report that the Federal commander, as many supposed Buell to be, was killed, and his body taken, revived the flagging hopes of the Confederates. Of the fluctuations of the battle from nine A.M. till three P.M. I can say but little, as it was mainly confined to our centre and left. During this time the Rebel forces had fallen back to the position occupied by Grant's advance Sabbath morning. The loyal troops had regained all the ground lost, and whatever of artillery and stores the Rebels had been unable to convey to the rear, and were now pressing us at every point.

Just before the retreat, occurred one of the most remarkable incidents of the battle; few more wonderful are on record. General Hindman, than whom no more fearless, dashing, or brave man is found in the Rebel service, was leading his men in a fearful struggle for the possession of a favourable position, when a shell from the Federal batteries, striking his horse in the breast and passing into his body, exploded. The horse was blown to fragments, and the rider, with his saddle, lifted some ten feet in the air. His staff did not doubt that their general was killed, and some one cried out, "General Hindman is blown to pieces." Scarcely was the cry uttered, when Hindman sprang to his feet and shouted, "Shut up there, I am worth two dead men yet. Get me another horse." To the amazement of every one, he was but little bruised. His heavy and strong cavalry saddle, and probably the bursting of the shell downward, saved him. In a minute he was on a new horse and rallying his men for another dash. A man of less flexible and steel-like frame would probably have been so jarred and stunned by the shock as to be unable to rise; he, though covered with blood and dust, kept his saddle during the remainder of the day, and performed prodigies of valour. But no heroism of officers or men could avail to stay the advance of the Federal troops.

At three o'clock P.M. the Confederates decided on a

retreat to Corinth; and General Breckenridge, strengthened by three regiments of cavalry,—Forrest's, Adams', and the Texas Rangers, raising his effective force to 12,000 men,—received orders to protect the rear. By four P.M. the Confederates were in full retreat. The main body of the army passed silently and swiftly along the road toward Corinth, our division bringing up the rear, determined to make a desperate stand if pursued. At this time the Union forces might have closed in upon our retreating columns and cut off Breckenridge's division, and perhaps captured it. A Federal battery threw some shells, as a feeler, across the road on which we were retreating, between our division and the main body, but no reply was made to them, as this would have betrayed our position. We passed on with little opposition or loss, and by five o'clock had reached a point one and a half miles nearer Corinth than the point of attack Sabbath morning.

Up to this time the pursuit seemed feeble, and the Confederates were surprised that the victorious Federals made no more of their advantage. Nor is it yet understood why the pursuit was not pressed. A rapid and persistent pursuit would have created a complete rout of the now broken, weary, and dispirited Rebels. Two hours more of such fighting as Buell's fresh men could have made, would have demoralized and destroyed Beauregard's army. For some reason this was not done, and night closed the battle.

About five o'clock I requested permission to ride on toward Corinth, as I was faint and weary, and, from the pain in my side and knee, would not be able to keep the saddle much longer. This was granted, and I made a detour from the road on which the army was retreating, that I might travel faster and get ahead of the main body. In this ride of twelve miles alongside of the routed army, I saw more of human agony and woe than I trust I will ever again be called on to witness. The retreating host wound along a narrow and almost impassable road, extending some seven or eight miles in length. Here was a long line of wagons loaded with wounded, piled in like bags of grain, groaning and cursing, while the mules plunged on in mud and water belly-deep, the water sometimes coming into the wagons. Next came a straggling regiment of infantry pressing on past the train of wagons, then a stretcher borne upon the shoulders of four men, carrying a wounded officer, then soldiers staggering along, with an arm broken and hanging down, or other fearful wounds which were enough to destroy life. And to add to the horrors of the scene, the elements of heaven marshalled their forces,—a fitting accompaniment of the tempest of human desolation and passion which was raging. A cold, drizzling rain commenced about nightfall, and soon came harder and faster, then turned to pitiless blinding hail. This storm raged with unrelenting violence for three hours. I passed long wagon trains filled with wounded and dying soldiers, without even a blanket to shield them from the driving sleet and hail, which fell in stones as large as partridge eggs, until it lay on the ground two inches deep.

Some three hundred men died during that awful retreat, and their bodies were thrown out to make room for others who, although wounded, had struggled on through the storm, hoping to find shelter, rest, and medical care.

By eight o'clock at night I had passed the whole retreating column, and was now in advance, hoping to reach Corinth, still four miles ahead. But my powers of endurance, though remarkable, were exhausted, and I dismounted at a deserted cabin by the wayside, scarce able to drag myself to the doorway. Here a surgeon was tending some wounded men who had been sent off the field at an early hour of the first day. To his question, "Are you wounded?" I replied that my wound was slight, and that I needed refreshment and sleep more than surgical aid. Procuring two hard crackers and a cup of rye coffee, I made a better meal than I had eaten in three days, and then lay down in a vacant room and slept.

When I awoke it was broad daylight, and the room was crowded full of wounded and dying men, so thickly packed that I could hardly stir. I was not in the same place where I had lain down; but of my change of place, and of the dreadful scenes which had occurred during the night, I had not the slightest knowledge.

As I became fully awake and sat up, the surgeon turned to me, and said, "Well, you are alive at last. I thought nothing but an earthquake would wake you. We have moved you about like a log, and you never groaned or showed any signs of life. Men have trampled on you, dying men have groaned all around you, and yet you slept as soundly as a babe in its cradle. Where is your wound?"

How I endured the horrors of that night, rather how I was entirely unconscious of them and slept refreshingly through them, is to me a mystery. But so it was, and it seemed to be the turning-point of my knee-wound, as it has never troubled me so much since.

I now rode on to Corinth, where I changed clothes, had a bath and breakfast, and found a hospital and a surgeon. He decided that I was unfit for duty, and must take my place among the invalids. After dressing my wounds he advised rest. I slept again for six hours, and woke in the afternoon almost a well man, as I thought.

Thus ended my courier service, and I then resolved that no earthly power should ever force me into another battle against the Government under which I was born; and I have kept my resolution.

General Beauregard's official dispatch of the second day's battle, given below, was a very neat attempt to cover up defeat. It expresses the general opinion of the people in the South as to the battle of Pittsburgh Landing.

Corinth, Tuesday,
April 8, 1862.

To the Secretary of War
Richmond:

We have gained a great and glorious victory. Eight to ten thousand prisoners, and thirty-six pieces of cannon. Buell reinforced Grant, and we retired to our entrenchments at Corinth, which we can hold. Loss heavy on both sides.

Beauregard

Chapter 6

Hospital Service

The wounded were now arriving in large numbers, but so exhausted by the loss of blood, the jolting in rough wagons, and the exposure of the fearful night, that many were too far gone for relief.

As I had, while at school in New York, frequented the hospitals, and also attended two courses of medical lectures, I had gained a little knowledge of wounds and their treatment. This fact, and a special fondness if not aptitude for that study, decided my future course.

My first care was for the members of the company I had commanded during the long retreat from Nashville; hence I went out to seek them. Meeting them a short distance from Corinth, I had them taken to a hospital established in an unfinished brick church in the north end of the town, and here I remained, giving them all possible care and attention.

Next morning, Dr. J.C. Nott, Surgeon-general of the Western division of the Confederate service, appointed me as assistant-surgeon on his staff. The scarcity of surgeons to meet the immense demand, and, perhaps, a little skill shown in dressing wounds, secured me this appointment. On the following Saturday, April 12, 1862, I obtained an honourable discharge from the army, on account of my wounds, but retained my position of assistant-surgeon, as a civilian appointment.

During the ten days I remained at Corinth the town was a perfect aceldama, though all was done that could be to save life and alleviate suffering. Many of the best surgeons in the South arrived in time to render valuable assistance to the army surgeons in their laborious duties. Among these may be named Surrell of Virginia, Hargis and Baldwin of Mississippi, Richardson of New Orleans, La Fressne of Alabama, with many others of high reputation. During the week following the battle the wounded were brought in by hundreds, and the surgeons were over tasked. Above 5000 wounded men, demanding instant and constant attendance, made a call too great to be met successfully. A much larger proportion of amputations was performed than would have been necessary if the wounds could have received earlier attention. On account of exposures, many wounds were gangrenous when the patients reached the hospital. In these cases delay was fatal, and an operation almost equally so, as tetanus often followed speedily. Where amputation was performed, eight out of ten died. The deaths in Corinth averaged fifty per day for a week after the battle. While the surgeons, as a body, did their duty nobly, there were some young men, apparently just out of college, who performed difficult operations with the assurance and assumed skill of practiced surgeons, and with little regard for human life or limb. In a few days erysipelas broke out, and numbers died of it. Pneumonia, typhoid fever, and measles followed, and Corinth was one entire hospital. As soon as possible, the wounded who could be moved were sent off to Columbus, Okalona, Lauderdale Springs, and elsewhere, and some relief was thus obtained. We were also comforted by the arrival of a corps of nurses. Their presence acted like a charm. Order emerged from chaos, and in a few hours all looked cleaner and really felt better, from the skill and industry of a few devoted women. A pleasant instance of the restraint of woman's presence upon the roughest natures occurred in the hospital I was attending. A stalwart backwoodsman was suffering from a broken arm, and had been venting his spleen upon the doctors and male nurses by continued profanity; but when one of his fellow-sufferers uttered an oath, while the "Sisters" were near ministering to the comfort of the wounded, he sharply reproved him, demanding—"Have you no more manners than to swear in the presence of ladies?" All honour to these devoted Sisters, who, fearless of danger and disease, sacrificed every personal comfort to alleviate the sufferings of the sick and wounded after this terrible battle.

An instance of most heroic endurance, if not of foolhardy stoicism, such as has few parallels in history, occurred during the contest, which deserves mention. Brigadier-general Gladden, of South Carolina, who was in General Bragg's command, had his left arm shattered by a ball, on the first day of the fight. Amputation was performed hastily by his staff-surgeon on the field; and then, instead of being taken to the rear for quiet and nursing, he mounted his horse, against the most earnest remonstrances of all his staff, and continued to command. On Monday, he was again in the saddle, and kept it during the day; on Tuesday, he rode on horseback to Corinth, twenty miles from the scene of action, and continued to discharge the duties of an officer. On Wednesday, a second amputation, near the shoulder, was necessary, when General Bragg sent an aid to ask if he would not be relieved of his command. To which he replied, "Give General Bragg my compliments, and say that General Gladden will only give up his command to go into his coffin." Against the remonstrances of personal friends, and the positive injunctions of the surgeons, he persisted in sitting up in his chair, receiving dispatches and giving directions, till Wednesday afternoon, when lockjaw seized him, and he died in a few moments. A sad end was this, for a man possessing many of the noblest and most exalted characteristics.

Two days thereafter, on the 11th of April, there was perpetrated one of the most diabolical murders ever sanctioned by the forms of law. It illustrates the atrocious wickedness of the rebellion, and the peril of sympathy with the Union cause in the South. Patriotism here wins applause, there a culprit's doom. The facts were these: When the Rebels were raising a force in Eastern Tennessee, two brothers by the name of Rowland volunteered; a younger brother, William H. Rowland, was a Union man, and refusing to enlist was seized and forced into the army. He constantly protested against his impressment, but without avail. He then warned them that he would desert the first opportunity, as he would not fight against the cause of right and good government. They were inexorable, and he was torn from his family and hurried to the field. At the battle of Fort Donelson, Rowland escaped from his captors in the second day's action, and immediately joined the loyal army. Though now, to fight against his own brothers, he felt that he was in a righteous cause, and contending for a worthy end.

In the battle of Pittsburgh Landing he was taken prisoner by the very regiment to which he had formerly belonged. This sealed his fate. On the way to Corinth several of his old comrades, among them his two brothers, attempted to kill him, one of them nearly running him through with a bayonet. He was, however, rescued from this peril by the guard. Three days after the retreating army had reached Corinth, General Hardee, in whose division was the regiment claiming this man as a deserter, gave orders to have Rowland executed. The general, I hope from some misgivings of conscience, was unwilling to witness the execution of his own order, and detailed General Claibourne to carry out the sentence. About four o'clock P.M., some 10,000 Tennessee troops were drawn up in two parallel lines, facing inward, three hundred yards apart. The doomed man, surrounded by the guard, detailed from his own former regiment to shoot him, marched with a firm step into the middle of the space between the two lines of troops. Here his grave had been already dug, and a black pine coffin lay beside it. No minister of religion offered to direct his thoughts to a gracious Saviour. I fear he was poorly prepared for the eternity upon which he was just entering.

The sentence was read, and he was asked if he had any thing to say why it should not be executed. He spoke in a firm, decided tone, in a voice which could be heard by many hundreds, and nearly in the following words. "Fellow-soldiers, Tennesseans, I was forced into Southern service against my will and against my conscience. I told them I would desert the first chance I found, and I did it. I was always a Union man and never denied it, and I joined the Union army to do all the damage I could to the Confederates. I believe the Union cause is right and will triumph. You can kill me but once, and I am not afraid to die in a good cause. My only request is, that you let my wife and family know that I died like a man in supporting my principles. My brothers there would shoot me if they had a chance, but I forgive them. Now shoot me through the heart, that I may die instantly."

Such were his fearless, even defiant words, and I recall them with the distinctness of a present thought, for it needed little imagination to place myself in his stead. Had I succeeded in escaping at any former period and been retaken, this would have been my fate. While I saw the hazard, I was none the less resolved to make the attempt, and soon.

After Rowland had ceased to speak, he took off hat, coat, and necktie, and laying his hand on his heart, he said, "Aim here." But the sergeant of the guard advanced to tie his hands and blindfold him. He asked the privilege of standing untied; the request was not granted. His eyes were then bandaged, he kneeled upon his coffin, and engaged in prayer for several minutes, and then said he was ready. The lieutenant of the guard then gave the word, "Fire," and twenty-four muskets, half of them loaded with ball, were discharged. When the smoke lifted, the body had fallen backward, and was still. Several balls had passed through his head, and some through his heart. His body was tumbled into the rough pine box, and buried by the men that shot him. Such was the fate of a Tennessee patriot. His blood will be required of those who instigated the Rebellion. General Hardee said afterward, when the scene was described to him, "I think the man was half crazy from brooding over his fancied wrongs. His execution was necessary to prevent others from deserting, but no sum of money could have induced me to witness it." General, were they "fancied wrongs!"

This scene strengthened my purpose to disconnect myself from the South as soon as I could get my pay, which was now many months in arrears. I could not travel many hundreds of miles without means, and in a direction to excite suspicion in the mind of every man I might meet.

But the paymaster was not in funds; and while he approved and indorsed my bills, he said I must go to Richmond to receive the money. I had not means to go to Richmond. My horses, of which I owned two, I was determined to keep, to aid me off; hence I was forced to continue in my position as assistant-surgeon for a time.

On the 17th of April, the surgeon-general to whose staff I was attached left Corinth for Mobile, nearly three hundred miles distant, with a train conveying about forty wounded men. The journey was tedious, and to the wounded, painful, as they occupied box-cars without springs, and the weather was exceedingly warm. A few of the men were left under the care of physicians by the way, being unable to endure the motion of the cars. We proceeded leisurely from station to station, stopping long enough to receive provisions for all on board from the citizens on the line of the road, which were freely and gratuitously furnished. Wherever we stopped long enough to give the people time to assemble, crowds came to offer relief,—ladies with flowers, jellies, and cakes for the poor fellows, and men with the more substantial provisions. One rich old gentleman at Lauderdale Springs, named Martin, sent in a wagon loaded with stores. This exuberance of supplies thus voluntarily furnished, is an index of the feeling of the masses in the South as to the cause in which they have embarked their all.

At the end of two and a half days we reached Mobile, and were met at the depot by a large company of ladies with carriages, to take the wounded men to a spacious and airy hospital, prepared with every necessary and comfort which could be devised. A large number of servants were in attendance, to carry those too severely wounded to ride in the carriages; and whatever water, and clean suits, and food, and smiles, and sympathy, and Christian conversation, and religious books, could do for their comfort, was done.

After seeing the men nicely cared for, and resting, I set myself to investigations as to the possibility of escape from Mobile out to the blockading fleet, in case I could not get my pay to go home by land. I met no cheering facts in this search. There were about 4000 troops in and around the city. Fort Morgan was strongly guarded, and egress was difficult, while the Union fleet lay far out. I gave this up, as not feasible for the present, at least.

Mobile was stagnant commercially, business at a standstill, many stores closed, and all looked gloomy. The arrival from Havana of a vessel which had eluded the blockading fleet, loaded with coffee, cigars, &c., produced a temporary and feeble excitement. But so frequent were these arrivals that the novelty had worn off: though in this fact I see no ground for reproaching either the heads of department at Washington or the commanders of the blockading squadron at that point. The whole coast is indented with bays, and interior lines of navigable water are numerous; so that nothing but a cordon of ships, in close proximity along the whole coast, could entirely forbid ingress and egress.

Another instance of the rigid surveillance of the press maintained in the Confederate States is suggested by this incident. The city papers of Mobile made no mention of this arrival, though all knew it. Early in the year, Southern papers boasted of the number of ships which accomplished the feat, giving names, places, and cargoes; but months ago this was forbidden, and wisely for their interests. Recently I have seen no mention in Southern papers of the importation of cannon or any thing else, except in purposely blind phrase as to time and place.

I returned to the hospital, feeling that my destinies were wrapped up with it for a while yet. Here I witnessed an illustration of the power of popular enthusiasm worthy of mention. A miserly old gentleman, who had never been known, it was said, to do a generous act, and who had thrown off all appeals for aid to ordinary benevolent causes with an imperative negative, was so overcome by the popular breeze in favour of the soldiers, that he came into the hospital with a roll of bank-bills in his hand, and passing from cot to cot gave each wounded man a five-dollar bill, repeating, with a spasmodic jerk of his head and a forced smile, "Make yourself comfortable; make yourself comfortable, my good fellow." I am afraid he, poor fellow, did not feel very comfortable, as his money was screwed out of him by the power of public opinion.

The Surgeon-general, a man as noble in private life as distinguished in his profession, asked me to take charge of a hospital at Selma, one hundred and eighty miles up the Alabama river, under the direction of Dr. W.P. Reese, post-surgeon; and on the 21st of April I left for that place, with twenty-three wounded men under my care. We reached the town the next day, my men improved by the river transit. Here we were again met by carriages, in readiness to convey the wounded to a hospital, fitted up in a large Female Seminary building, admirably adapted for the purpose, with spacious rooms, high ceilings, and well ventilated. One wing of this building, containing a large music-room, was appropriated to my charge. The sick men of a regiment organizing there, occupied another part of the building. The school, like so many others in the South, was scattered by the war.

Here again we were burdened with kindness from the ladies. Wines, jellies, strawberries, cakes, flowers, were always abundant, served by beautiful women, with the most bewitching smiles. I had been so long cut off from refined female society, that I appreciated most profoundly their kind attentions. So intent were they upon contributing to the comfort of the men who had been wounded in protecting their homes, as they regarded it, that they brought a piano into my ward, and the young ladies vied with each other in delectating us with the Marseillaise, Dixie, and like patriotic songs, interspersing occasionally something about moonlight walks in Southern bowers, &c, which my modesty would not allow me to suppose had any reference to the tall young surgeon.

Selma is a beautiful town of three or four thousand inhabitants, situated on the right bank of the Alabama river, on a level plateau, stretching off from the bank, which rises from forty to fifty feet above the river by a steep ascent. A distinguishing feature of the place is its Artesian wells, said to be equal to any in the world. In the main street of the town, at the crossing of other streets, are reservoirs, five in number, which receive the water thrown up from a depth of many hundred feet, and in quantity far beyond the demands of the inhabitants. The water is slightly impregnated with mineral qualities, is pleasant to the taste, and regarded as medicinal. The people of Selma are generally highly intelligent and refined, and no more pleasant acquaintances did I form in the South than here. Their zeal for the Rebel cause was up to fever heat, and their benevolence for its soldiers without stint. The provisions for the hospital were furnished gratuitously by a committee of the Relief Association, and they appeared grieved that we made no more demands upon them. That my hospital was a model of neatness and perfection in its line, was attested by a report of Adjutant-general Cooper, who visited incognito the hospitals through the South while I was at Selma. He gave it the preference over all he had seen, in a publication which appeared shortly after this time in the Southern papers.

At the end of three weeks of attendance here, I obtained a furlough for ten days, that I might go to Richmond to secure my pay. Securing government transportation, I reached Richmond on the 15th of May, exceedingly anxious to find the quartermaster in an amiable mood and in funds; for upon my success here depended my hopes of a speedy escape. Money will often accomplish what daring would not. But here I was disappointed—at least partially. I secured but one-fifth of my claim, which was admitted without question; but I was told that the quartermaster of the Western division had funds, and I must get the remainder there. My remonstrances availed nothing, and I left the office in no amiable mood.

I now determined to avenge myself upon a faithless government, by acquiring all possible information of the status of the Rebel army in and about Richmond, which might be of use to me and my country. In this I also failed, from the exceeding, and, I must say, wise vigilance of the authorities. My pass to enter the city allowed nothing further—I must procure one to remain in the city, and this was called for at almost every street corner; and then another to leave the city, and only in one direction.

Although I appeared in the dress of an assistant-surgeon, with the M.S. upon my cap, I could gain no access to the army outside of the city, nor make any headway in my tour of observation; and as they charged me five dollars per day at the Ballard House, I must soon leave, or be swamped. I had not been so completely foiled in my plans hitherto.

I left Richmond for Selma the 20th of May, reflecting bitterly upon the character of a rebellion which, commenced in fraud, was perpetuating itself by forcing its enemies to fight their own friends, and then refused to pay them the stipulated price of their enforced service. The longer I reflected, the more fully was I convinced that I never would receive my pay. The conscription act, which took effect the 16th of May, was being enforced with a sweeping and searching universality. If I returned to Corinth to seek the quartermaster there, the payment would be deferred, from one excuse or another, until I should be forced into the service again. The thought that the Rebel authorities were breaking their pledges to pay me, that they might get their hated coils around me once more, from which I had but partially extricated myself, almost maddened me. I knew, moreover, that I could not long remain in Selma, in my present situation. The men were all recovering, except one poor fellow, who soon passed beyond the reach of earthly mutilations, and no new shipments of wounded were coming on. And the force of public opinion in Selma was such, that no man able to fight could remain there. The unmarried ladies were so patriotic, that every able-bodied young man was constrained to enlist. Some months previous to this, a gentleman was known to be engaged for an early marriage, and hence declined to volunteer. When his betrothed, a charming girl and a devoted lover, heard of his refusal, she sent him, by the hand of a slave, a package inclosing a note. The package contained a lady's skirt and crinoline, and the note these terse words: "Wear these, or volunteer." He volunteered.

When will the North wake up to a true and manly patriotism in the defence of their national life, now threatened by the tiger-grasp of this atrocious Rebellion? Hundreds upon hundreds of young men I see in stores and shops, doing work that women could do quite as well; and large numbers of older men who have grown wealthy under the protection of our benign government, are idly grieving over the taxation which the war imposes, and meanly asking if it will not soon end, that their coffers may become plethoric of gold; while the question is still unsettled whether the Rebellion shall sweep them and their all into the vortex of ruin and anarchy. The North is asleep! and it will become the sleep of death, national death, if a new spirit be not speedily awaked!

CHAPTER 7

My Escape

It was now evident that I could not avoid the conscription if I remained longer, and yet I could not secure my pay; and how could I travel hundreds of miles without means? I would have sold one of my horses, but prices were low at Selma, far away from the seat of war, and the pay must be in Confederate money, which was of little value. This sacrifice I was unwilling to make, especially as I might need every dollar I could procure to help me out of Dixie. Other obstacles lay across the pathway of escape. Every military point was guarded, and every railroad and public highway under military control. It was hence impossible for me to escape, travelling in citizen's dress; and yet I had no military commission, having left the service when I entered the hospital. I resolved to retain my officer's cap and martial uniform, and travel as a Confederate officer on furlough, and if not questioned too closely might succeed.

On the morning of May 26th I had made all the arrangements possible for the welfare of my patients, and passing through I looked each in the face, as a kindly farewell on my part, to which they might return their adieu some days after, when they "found me missing." I charged young Dr. Reese to take good care of the men till I returned, as I thought of taking my horses up the Alabama river to place them on a farm for pasture. Taking a last look at the beautiful town of Selma, with a suppressed sigh that I should no more enjoy the society of its fair ladies, I embarked on the *Great Republic* for Montgomery, the capital of the State, and for a time the capital of the Confederacy. I reached this point in the evening, having made sixty-five miles toward the north star. I remained at Montgomery over night, and managed to obtain a military pass and transportation from this point to Chattanooga, which was now in possession of a large force of Confederate cavalry, organizing themselves into guerrilla bands, while the Federal forces held the north side of the Tennessee. While here it seemed necessary to exchange my Confederate money into gold, as the only sure means of paying my way when I should reach the Federal lines. But this was not easily effected. The Confederates sent their gold to Europe by millions to buy arms and munitions of war, relying upon the patriotism of the people to keep up the credit of the national currency; and lest brokers should undertake to depreciate it, they passed a law imposing a heavy penalty upon any one who should discount Confederate notes. For a time this succeeded in keeping up the credit of the circulating medium; but all gold disappeared, and silver change was unknown. But as I must have gold, I walked into a broker's office and stated that I wished to purchase seven ounces of gold, and exhibited a roll of Confederate notes. After a little figuring, he said seven ounces would cost me two hundred and seventy dollars of my money. I replied, "Weigh it out."

"Bullion or coin?"

I answered that coin was more convenient to carry. The

coin was weighed, and I retired, wondering if anybody had broken the law forbidding the discount of Confederate scrip.

After leaving Montgomery by the railroad train for Chattanooga on the morning of the 27th, I fell in with a soldier whose name I must for the sake of his family, who showed me great kindness, conceal. He said he was going home on furlough. As I then suspected and afterward learned, he was deserting, while I was escaping. A fellow-feeling, though at first unconfessed to each other, drew us together, and at length I learned his whole history. My greater caution and accustomed reticence, gave him but a meagre idea of my adventures or purposes. His story, reaffirmed to me when near death some weeks later, is worth recital, especially as it illustrates both the strength of the Rebel Government, and the desperate lengths to which they go in pressing men into the service.

The conscription act passed by the Confederate Congress went into operation on May 16th, 1862. By this law all able-bodied white male citizens, between the ages of eighteen and thirty-five, were actually taken into the service; that is, they were taken from their homes, placed in camps of instruction, and forwarded to the armies in the field as fast as needed. Another clause of the act required the enrolling of all between the ages of thirty-five and fifty-five years, as a reserve militia, to serve in their own State in case of invasion. As their States have all been "invaded," this virtually sweeps into the Southern army all white men able to bear arms between eighteen and fifty-five years of age. Another clause provided that all persons then in the army, under eighteen and over thirty-five, might return home discharged from the service within ninety days after the act took effect, provided, their regiments were filled up with conscripts. By this provision the regiments would be kept full. Still another clause directed that the twelve-months men now in the service, should "be allowed" (i.e., required), "at the expiration of their twelve months to elect new officers, and take the oath for two years or the war." Under this last clause, the reorganization of the twelve-months volunteers was going forward at Corinth, when the Fifth Tennessee regiment of volunteers, composed of Warren county boys, Colonel J.B. Hill commanding, determined they would not be forced to continue their service, and especially out of their own State. Before this determination had entirely taken form the officers were apprised of the disaffection, and resolved, with true military decision, to forestall the threatened mutiny. The regiment was marched out some distance from camp and drilled for an hour or two, and then allowed to stack arms and return to camp for dinner. While in camp their arms were removed, and 30,000 men drawn up: 15,000 on each side of a hollow square, with a battery of ten field-pieces loaded with grape, gunners at their post, occupying a third side, while the fourth was open. Into this space the regiment was marched, without arms, and requested, all of them who were free to do so, to take the oath. After its administration to the regiment in a body, the colonel said if there were any members who had not voluntarily sworn, they could step out in front of the ranks. Six men advanced, two of them brothers, and remonstrated that they had cheerfully volunteered for one year, had served faithfully, and endured every hardship without complaint and without furlough; had left their families without means of support, who must now be suffering; that if allowed to go home and rest and make some provision for wife and children, they would then return.

Colonel Hill, who was from the neighbourhood of these men, knew the truth and felt the force of their arguments, and was trying by kindness to satisfy their minds, when General Beauregard rode up and asked—

"Colonel Hill, do these men refuse to swear?"

"Yes, sir."

"Unless they comply, have them shot to-morrow morning at ten o'clock," said the general, and rode away.

Before ten o'clock they had all taken the oath; but one of the two brothers, in his rage, declared he would desert. For this he would have been shot, had he not acknowledged himself wrong and professed penitence, though his resolution remained unshaken.

Some days after, this brother was placed upon picket duty, and, as the night came on, he attempted to pass out through the lines of cavalry pickets, when he was shot in the side, but not dangerously wounded as he then thought. He crawled back into his own line, and then reported himself as shot by a Federal picket. He was taken to camp, the ball extracted, and he sent to Atlanta, Georgia, to hospital. From this place he escaped and reached Montgomery on his way back to Warren county, Tennessee. His wound healed externally.

This was the deserting soldier I met on the cars as we left Montgomery for Chattanooga. I put him in temporary possession of one of my horses; we united our destinies, and prepared for the future as well as we could.

We reached Chattanooga on June 1st, and I found it, to my chagrin, a military camp, containing 7,500 cavalry, under strict military rule. We were now in a trap, as our pass here ended, and we were near the Federal lines. How to get out of the town was now the problem, and one of the most difficult I had yet met in my study of Rebel topography.

We put up at the Crutchfield House, stabled our horses, and sat about in the bar-room, saying nothing to attract attention, but getting all the information possible. I was specially careful not to be recognized. The cavalry company I had commanded on the long retreat from Nashville, was in Chattanooga at this time. Had any one of them seen me, my position would have been doubly critical; as it was, I felt the need of circumspection. It was clear to me that we could not leave Chattanooga in military garb, as we had entered it, for, without a pass, no cavalryman could leave the lines. This settled, a walk along the street, showed me a Jew clothing-store, with suits new and old, military and agricultural. My resolution was formed, and I went to the stable, taking with me a newly fledged cavalry officer, who needed and was able to pay for an elegant cavalry saddle. Being "hard up" for cash, I must sell: and he flush of money and pride, must buy. Thus I was rid of one chief evidence of the military profession. A small portion of the price purchased a plain farmer-like saddle and bridle. An accommodating dealer in clothes next made me look quite like a country farmer of the middle class. My companion was equally successful in transforming himself, and in the dusk of the evening we were passing out to the country as farmers who had been in to see the sights.

We safely reached and passed the outer pickets, and then took to the woods, and struck in toward the Tennessee river, hoping to find a ferry where money, backed, if necessary, by the moral suasion of pistols, would put us across. I was growing desperate, and determined not to be foiled. We made some twelve miles, and then rested in the woods till morning, when selecting the safest hiding-place I could find, I left my companion with the horses and started out on a reconnaissance.

Trudging along a road in the direction of the river, I met a guileless man who gave me some information of the name and locality of a ferryman, who had formerly acted in that capacity, though now no one was allowed to cross. Carefully noting all the facts I could draw out of this man, I strolled on and soon fell in with another, and gained additional light, one item of which was that the old "flat" lay near, and just below, the ferryman's house. Thus enlightened, I walked on and found the house and my breakfast. Being a traveller, I secured without suspicion sandwiches enough to supply my companion with dinner and supper, which he enjoyed as he took care of the horses in the woods. A circuitous route brought me to them, and I was pleased to see the horses making a good meal from the abundant grass. This was an important point, as our lives might yet depend upon their speed and endurance.

I laid before my companion the rather dubious prospect, that the orders were strict that no man should be ferried across the river; the ferryman was faithful to the South; he had been conscientious in his refusal to many applications; no sum would induce him to risk his neck, &c. All this I had heard from his lips, backed with a *quantum sufficit* of oaths, which for once I was rather willing to hear, having already learned that the man who accompanies his statements with a gratuitous and profuse profanity, is not usually brave to make them good when the trial comes. To his boastful words that "no white-livered traitor to the Southern cause should ever cross that ferry to give information to the Yankees," I fully assented, and advised him, to be doubly on his guard, as the Federals were not far off, not hinting that I wanted to cross. Yet my purpose was formed: we must cross the river that night, and this man must take us over, as there was no other hope of escape. Having laid the plan before my companion, as evening drew on I again sought the cabin of the retired ferryman. My second appearance was explained by the statement that I had got off the road, and wandering in the woods, had come round to the same place. This was literally true, though I must admit it did not give to him an impression of the whole truth. A rigid casuist might question the truthfulness of my statement to the Secession ferryman; but a man fleeing for his life, and hunted by a relentless enemy, has not much time to settle questions in casuistry.

After taking supper with the ferryman, we walked out smoking and chatting. By degrees I succeeded in taking him down near the ferry, and there sat down on the bank to try the effect upon his avaricious heart of the sight of some gold which I had purchased at Montgomery. His eyes glistened as he examined an eagle with unwonted eagerness, while we talked of the uncertain value of paper-money, and the probable future value of Confederate scrip.

As the time drew near when my companion, according to agreement, was to ride boldly to the river, I stepped down to take a look at his unused flat. He, of course, walked with me. While standing with my foot upon the end of his boat, I heard the tramp of the horses, and said to him, in a quiet tone—"Here is an eagle; you must take me and my companion over." He remonstrated, and could not risk his life for that, &c. Another ten dollars was demanded and paid, the horses were in the flat, and in two minutes we were off for—home.

During that dark and uncertain voyage, I had time not only to coax into quietness my restive horse, but also to conclude that it would never do to dismiss our Charon on the other bank, as half an hour might put on our track a squad of cavalry, who, in our ignorance of the roads and country, would soon return us to Rebeldom and a rope. A man who would take twenty dollars for twenty minutes' work, after swearing that his conscience would not allow him to disobey the authorities, was not to be trusted out of your sight. Standing near my companion, I whispered—"This man must pilot us to some point you will know." I should have stated that this deserting soldier was within sixty miles of his home, and had some knowledge of the localities not far north from our present position. With this purpose, I arranged, when we touched the bank, to be in the rear of the ferryman, and followed him as he stepped off the boat, to take breath before a return pull. "Now, my good fellow," said I, "you have done us one good turn for pay, you must do another for friendship. We are strangers here, and you must take us to the foot of Waldon's Ridge, and then we will release you." To this demand he demurred most vigorously; but my determined position between him and the boat, gentle words, and an eloquent exhibition of my six-shooter, the sheen of which the moonlight enabled him to perceive, soon ended the parley, and onward he moved. We kept him in the road slightly ahead of us, with our horses on his two flanks, and chatted as sociably as the circumstances would permit. I am not careful to justify this constrained service exacted of the ferryman, further than to say, that I was now visiting upon the head, or rather the legs, of a real Secessionist, for an hour or two, just what for many months they had inflicted upon me. For six long miles we guarded our prisoner-pilot, and, reaching the foot of the mountain, the summit of which would reveal to my friend localities which he could recognize, and from which he could tell our bearings and distances, we called a halt. After apologizing for our rudeness on the plea of self-preservation, and thanking him for his enforced service, we bade him good-night, not doubting that he would reach the river in time to ferry himself over before daylight, and console his frightened wife by the sight of the golden bribe.

We were now, at eleven o'clock at night, under the shadow of a dark mountain, and with no knowledge of the course we were to take, other than the general purpose of pressing northward.

After making some miles of headway and rising several hundred feet, we struck off at a right angle from the road, worked our way for a mile among the rocks, and tying our horses, lay down under an overhanging cliff and tried to sleep. But I wooed Somnus in vain. My brain and heart were too full. On the verge of a Canaan, for which I had looked and struggled daring thirteen wearisome months, would I now reach it in peace, or must other perils be encountered, and I perhaps thrust back into a dungeon to meet a deserter's fate? The future was still uncertain, and my mind turned backward, recalling childhood's joys and a mother's undying love. Oh, how I longed for one gentle caress from her soft hand to soothe me into sleep, and how vividly came back to my memory words committed long ago,—words which, with slight change, tenderly expressed the longing of my spirit that night. I sank into forgetfulness, repeating over and over those sweet strains:

Backward, turn backward,
O Time, in your flight;
Make me a child again, just for to-night!
Mother, come back from the far-distant shore,
Take me again to your heart as of yore;
Over my slumbers your loving watch keep,—

Rock me to sleep, mother—rock me to sleep.

Backward, flow backward,
O tide of the years!
I am so weary of toils and of tears,
Toil without recompense,—tears all in vain,—
Take them, and give me my childhood again.
I have grown weary of dust and decay,
Weary of flinging my soul-wealth away,
Weary of sowing for others to reap,—
Rock me to sleep, mother—rock me to sleep.

Tired of the hollow, the base, the untrue,
Mother, O mother, my heart calls for you.
Two weary summers the grass has grown green,
Blossomed, and faded, our faces between;
Yet with strong yearning and passionate pain,
Long I to-night for your presence again;
Come from the silence so long and so deep,—
Rock me to sleep, mother—rock me to sleep.

Over my heart in days that are flown,
No love like mother-love ever has shone;
No other fondness abides and endures,
Faithful, unselfish, and patient, like yours.
None like a mother can charm away pain
From the sick soul and the world-weary brain;
Slumber's soft dews o'er my heavy lids creep,—
Rock me to sleep, mother—rock me to sleep.

Come, let your brown hair, lighted with gold,
Fall on your shoulders again as of old;
Let it fall over my forehead to-night,
Shading my eyes from the moon's pallid light,
For with its sunny-edged shadows once more
Happily throng the sweet visions of yore;

Lovingly, softly its bright billows sweep,—
Rock me to sleep, mother—rock me to sleep.

Mother, dear mother, the years have been long,
Since last I was hushed by your lullaby song;
Sing then, and unto my soul it shall seem
That the years of my boyhood have been but a dream;
Clasp your lost son in a loving embrace,
Your love-lighted lashes just sweeping my face,
Never hereafter to part or to weep,—
Rock me to sleep, mother—rock me to sleep.

On the morning of June the third the sun rose beautifully over the Cumberland Mountains, flooding the valley of the Sequatchie, as we descended into it with lighter hearts than we had felt for many a day. As we rode down the mountain, my companion recognized the localities in the distance, and described the route which, in so many miles, would bring us to his father's house. His side hurt him severely that day, as the hardships of the way had given him a cold, which threatened to inflame and reopen the wound he had received in attempting to escape through the cavalry picket. He talked much of home, and was sure his mother could cure him. Poor fellow! he was already beyond his mother's help, though I did not then suspect it.

By nine o'clock we reached a farm-house, whose inmates, without many troublesome inquiries, agreed to feed our half-starved horses and give us some breakfast. My noble Selim sorely needed food and grooming, and I could not but wish for a few days of rest for him. He had been my companion in many a wild dash, and had learned to respond to my patting of his finely-arched neck with a pricking up of his ears and a toss of his head, as much as to say, "I am ready." When first I formed Selim's acquaintance he was wild and self-willed, and, as already related, gave me a blow upon the knee from which I have not yet entirely recovered. But I had long ago forgiven him this unkindness, for he had carried me through all that terrible retreat from Nashville, had never failed me when a hard and hazardous scout was on hand, had stood quietly at Corinth while I lost two of his companions on the battle-field of Shiloh, and then, as if grateful that I had saved him from their fate, he ever after served me with entire docility. At Selma he bore me on many a pleasant jaunt beside some fair one of that pleasant town, and now he was with proud step bearing me toward my long-desired home. Did he not deserve my special care?'

Everybody we met was Secession, and took for granted we were. Was I not demonstrating my sentiments, by seceding from a government which affirmed the right in its fundamental law?

By the way, if the South could make good their present effort for an independent national existence, they would immediately change that provision by which they allow each State to withdraw at pleasure. The impression among the thinking minds with them is already fixed, that the principle is destructive of all permanent national authority, and existence even. A practical and almost fatal illustration of the principle of secession was given at Corinth just after the battle of Shiloh.

The Arkansas authorities, fearing the power of the Federal forces, required all the troops from their State to return home and protect their own citizens. General Hindman, who commanded the Arkansas troops, was in favour of returning to their own State; but Beauregard, as commander-in-chief of the Western army, resisted the demand. Excitement ran high, and mutiny was imminent for some days. Nothing but the resolute bearing of General Beauregard, threatening to shoot the first man who should attempt to leave, saved the Rebel army from destruction; for if the troops of one State had been allowed to withdraw on the plea of protecting their own borders, why should not all? This was well-understood, and hence resisted resolutely and successfully. At a later day, and as if in pursuance of a general plan, the Arkansas troops did go home; and thus they avoided a mutiny, which, had it been fully developed, would have involved at least 10,000 men. So rigid is the surveillance of the press, that no publication, so far as I know, was ever made of this affair, which threatened the disintegration of the whole Rebel army.

To return, we made some thirty miles, and ascending the Cumberland range in the evening, we again sought rest among the rocks. This we judged safest, since we knew not who might have seen us during the day, of an inquiring state of mind, as to our purpose and destination.

On the morning of June 4th, by a detour to conceal the course from which we came, and a journey of a dozen of miles, we reached the home of my wounded friend. I shall not attempt to describe his tearful, joyful meeting with his mother and three sisters, and the pride of the good old father as he folded his soldier-boy to his heart. My own emotions fully occupied me while their greetings lasted. I thought of my own fond mother, who had not heard from me for more than a year, and was perhaps then mourning me as dead, perchance had gone herself to the tomb in grief for the loss of her first-born son; of my reverend father, whose wise counsel I had often needed and longed for; of my sweet sisters and little brother, who every day wondered if their big brother still lived and would ever come home.

After a kindly greeting to the stranger who had brought home their wounded son, for they never suspected either that he had deserted or that I was escaping to the hated Yankees, they introduced me to all the comforts of their pleasant dwelling; and for the first time for many months I began to feel somewhat secure. Yet they were all Secessionists, and talked constantly of the success of the cause, and I must, of necessity, conceal my views and plans.

The day after our arrival, the wounded soldier took to his bed and never rose again. The hardships he had endured in the journey home, acting upon a system enfeebled by his wound, terminated in inflammation of the lungs, which within a week ended his life. I watched by his bed, nursed him carefully, and told him what little I knew of the better world, trying to recall all the sweet words of comfort I had heard pious people pour into the ears of dying ones in my childhood, when my father, as pastor, was often called to such scenes. I was not an experienced counsellor, but I knew there was One Name of sovereign power. That Name I told him of as best I could. About the 12th of June he passed into the Dark Beyond.

After the funeral ceremonies wore over, a letter came from the other brother, detailing the manner in which they had been compelled to swear in for the war, and saying that he would soon be home. He had not reached when I left there. I fear he failed in his attempt.

But one more step was needed to make me safe; that was, to get within the Federal lines, take the oath of allegiance, and secure a pass. But how could this be accomplished? Should the Federal authorities suspect me of having been in the Rebel service, would they allow me to take the oath and go my way? I knew not; but well I knew the Confederate officers were never guilty of such an absurdity. Judging others by themselves, they put little confidence in the fact that A.B. has sworn to this or that; and hence they watch him as carefully after as before. The North should know that oaths taken by Southerners before provost-marshals, in recovered cities such as Memphis, Nashville, &c, are not taken to be observed, as a general rule. They are taken as a matter of necessity, and with a mental reservation, that when the interests of their State demands, they are freed from the obligation. That this is a startling statement I admit, and if called on for the proof I might find it difficult to produce it; and yet from what I saw and heard scores of times, and in different parts of the South, I know it to be indubitably true.

An incident which occurred about the 20th of June, both endangered my escape and yet put me upon the way of its accomplishment. I rode my pet Selim into the village of McMinnville, a few miles from the place of my sojourn, to obtain information as to the proximity of the Federal forces, and, if possible, devise a plan of getting within their lines without exciting suspicion. As Selim stood at the hotel, to the amazement of every one, General Dumont's cavalry galloped into town, and one of the troopers taking a fancy to my horse, led him off without my knowledge, and certainly without my consent. My only consolation was, that my noble Selim was now to do service in the loyal ranks. My best wish for my good steed is, that he may carry some brave United States officer over the last prostrate foe of this ever-glorious Union.

The cavalry left the town in a few hours, after erecting a flag-staff and giving the Stars and Stripes to the breeze. Within a few days a squad of Morgan's cavalry came in, cut down the staff, and one of them rolling up the flag and strapping it behind his saddle, left word where General Dumont could see the flag if he chose to call.

I left soon after the Federals did, but in an opposite direction, with my final plan perfected. Spending two or three days more with my kind friends on the farm, I saddled my remaining horse, and telling the family I might not return for some time, I rode through McMinnville, and then direct for Murfreesboro, at that time in possession of the Union forces. When hailed by the pickets, a mile from the town, I told them I wished to see the officer in command. They directed me where to find him, and allowed me to advance. They knew far less of Southern cunning than I did, or they would not have allowed me to ride into the town without a guard. When I found the officer, I stated that some Federal cavalry had taken my horse in McMinnville a few days ago, and I wished to recover him. He told me he could give me no authority to secure my horse, unless I would take the oath of allegiance to the United States. To this I made no special objection. With a seeming hesitation, that I might wake up no suspicion of being different from the masses of farmers in that region, and yet with a joy that was almost too great to be concealed, I solemnly subscribed the following oath:

"I, A—— B——, solemnly swear, without any mental reservation or evasion, that I will support the Constitution of the United States and the laws made in pursuance thereof; and that I will not take up arms against the United States, or give aid or comfort, or furnish information, directly or indirectly, to any person or persons belonging to any of the so-styled Confederate States who are now or may be in rebellion against the United States. So help me God."

The other side of the paper contained a military pass, by authority of Lieutenant-colonel J.G. Parkhurst, Military Governor of Murfreesboro. I regarded myself as free from any possible obligation to the Confederates when discharged from their service on account of my wounds at Corinth. In voluntarily taking this oath, I trust I had some just sense of its awful solemnity, for I have never been able to look upon the appeal to God in this judicial form as a light matter. How good men can, satisfy their consciences for the deliberate violation of the oaths which so many of them have deliberately taken to support the Constitution of the United States, I know not. I know what they say in self-defence, for I have often listened to their special pleading. The premise, as my good Professor Owen of the Free Academy would term it—the foundation falsehood—of the whole Secession movement, is the doctrine of State Rights, as held by the South. "I owe allegiance to my State, and, when it commands, obedience to the United States." This idea has complete possession of the leading minds, and a belief in it accounts for the conduct of many noble men, who resisted Secession resolutely until their State was carried for the Rebellion. Whenever a State act was passed they yielded, and the people were a unit.

In addition to this fundamental error, they aver that they are engaged in a revolution, not a rebellion; and that the right of revolution is conceded, even by the North, now endeavouring to force them back into an oppressive and hated union; and that if we justify our fathers in forswearing allegiance to the British crown, we should not condemn the South in refusing obedience to a Union already dissolved. If this were as good an argument

as it is a fallacious one, ignoring as it does the total dis-
similarity in the two cases, and assuming falsely that the
Union is already dissolved, it fails to justify the individual
oath-breaking of many of the leaders in the revolt. They
swore to support the Constitution of the United States
at the very time they were meaning to destroy it. Some
of them took the oath as Cabinet officers and members
of Congress, that they might have the better opportunity
to overthrow the government. The truth must be admitted—and here lies the darkest blot upon the characters
of the arch-conspirators—they know not the sanctity of
an oath, nor regard its solemn pledges and imprecations.
They have shown, it has been eloquently said, the utmost
recklessness respecting the oath of allegiance to the nation. Men who sneered at the North as teaching a higher
law to God which should be paramount to all terrene
statutes, have been themselves among the first to hold
the supreme law of the land and their oath of fealty and
loyalty to that land, abrogated by the lower law of State
claims and State interests. It could not be sin in the man
of the North, if God and his country ever clashed, to say,
that well as he loved his country, he loved his God yet
more. But what plea shall shield the sin which claims to
love one's own petty State better than either country or
God? They have virtually tunnelled and honey-combed
into ruin the fundamental obligations of the citizen. Jesu-
itism had made itself a name of reproach by the doctrine
of mental reservation, under which the Jesuit held himself absolved from oaths of true witness-bearing, which
he at any time had taken to the nation and to God, if the
truth to be told harmed the interests of his own order,
whose interests he must shield by a silent reservation.
The lesser caste, the ecclesiastical clique, thus was held

paramount to the entire nation; and oaths of fidelity to the religious order, a mere handful of God's creatures, rode over the rights of the God whose name had been invoked to witness truth-telling, and over the rights of God's whole race of mankind, to have the truth told in their courts by those who had solemnly proclaimed and deliberately sworn that they would tell and were telling it. The State loyalty as being a mental reservation evermore to abrogate the oath of National loyalty:—what is it but a modern reproduction of the old Jesuit portent?

But perjury however palliated, and whether in Old World despots or in New World anarchists, involves, in the dread language of Scripture, the being "clothed with cursing as with a garment." That terrible phrase of inspiration describes, we suppose, not merely profuse profanity, but the earthly deception which attracts the heavenly malediction, the reply of a mocked God to a defiant transgressor, vengeance invoked, and the invocation answered. "*So help me God!*" is a phrase so often heard in jury-boxes and custom-houses, beside the ballot-box, and in the assumption of each civil office, that we do not at all times gauge its dread depth of meaning. It is not a mere prayer of help to tell the truth, but like the kindred Hebrew words, "So do God to me and more also!" it is an invocation of His vengeance and an abjuration of all His further favour if we palter with the truth. It means, "If I speak not truly and mean not sincerely, so do I forswear and renounce henceforth all help from God. I hope not His help in the cares of life. I hope not His help for the pardon of sin. I ask not His grace,—nor hope from His smile in death,—nor help at His hand into His eternal and holy heavens. All the aid man needs to ask, all the aid which God has to the asking heretofore lent, I distinctly surrender, if He the truth-seeing sees me now truth-wresting." Now the risk of trifling with such a thunderbolt is not small. The many noble, excellent, and Christian men, who may have been heedlessly involved in this Rebellion, in spite of past oaths to the nation, it is not our task to judge. But the act itself, of disregarding such sworn loyalty to their whole country,—the act in its general principles apart from all personal partakers in it,—we may and we must ponder. Now in this respect, if these views of our national oaths be just, our present Rebellion has not been merely treasonable, but its cradle-wrappings, its very swaddling-bands, have been manifold layers of perjury,—its infancy has been "clad with cursing as with a garment." Can a jealous God consolidate and perpetuate a power commenced in perjury?

After taking the oath, I told the officer that there were from seven to ten thousand Rebel cavalry at Chattanooga, a detachment of whom would surprise him some morning if he was not wide awake.

Having performed this first loyal act under my oath, I went out in search of Selim. He was not to be found in Murfreesboro, and a further search would have consumed time and thrown me back toward the Rebel lines. Overjoyed at my escape from the last danger, and not reluctant to make this contribution to the cause of my country, I turned my now buoyant steps homeward, under the protection of the Stars and Stripes. I rode into Nashville the 28th of June, with feelings widely different from those which crowded my breast when four months before I had ridden out of it in the rear of General Johnson's retreating army. I was then, though pleased with the excitement and dash of cavalry service, in a cause where my heart was not, in a retreat from my own friends, and becoming daily more identified in the minds of others with the Rebellion; now I was free from its trammels, with my face toward my long-lost home, with a wish in my heart, which has grown more intense daily, to aid my country in her perilous struggle.

A few hours at Nashville enabled me to see my father's friend, who had treated me so kindly when sick, and again thank him for his good deeds, and then I left for home.

I will not ask the reader to follow me in my rapid journey through Louisville and Cincinnati, and thence to New York. Nor need I describe my joyful, tearful, welcome reception by father, mother, sisters, and brother, as of one alive from the dead.

The story of my life in secessiondom is ended. If the foregoing pages, beside depicting my personal experience, have given any facts of value to my bleeding country—facts as to the diabolical barbarism of Southern society in trampling upon all personal rights—facts showing the intense and resolute earnestness of the whole Southern people in the Rebellion—facts demonstrating the large resources of the Rebels in arms and men, and the absolute military despotism which has combined and concentrated their power—facts of the atrocious character of the guerrilla system organized and legalized among them—facts exhibiting the efficiency of every arm of their military service—facts showing the necessity of restrictions upon the freedom of the press in times of war—facts revealing the demoralizing influence of the doctrine of State Rights in nullifying national fealty, and disregarding the sanctities of an oath—facts which, if universally known and duly regarded, would stir the North to a profounder sense of the desperate and deadly struggle in which they are engaged than they have ever yet felt—then my time and labour will not have been spent in vain.

LEONAUR

ALSO FROM LEONAUR
AVAILABLE IN SOFTCOVER OR HARDCOVER WITH DUST JACKET

CAPTAIN OF THE 95th (Rifles) *by Jonathan Leach*—An officer of Wellington's Sharpshooters during the Peninsular, South of France and Waterloo Campaigns of the Napoleonic Wars.

THE KHAKEE RESSALAH *by Robert Henry Wallace Dunlop*—Service & adventure with the Meerut volunteer horse during the Indian mutiny 1857-1858

BUGLER AND OFFICER OF THE RIFLES *by William Green & Harry Smith* With the 95th (Rifles) during the Peninsular & Waterloo Campaigns of the Napoleonic Wars

BAYONETS, BUGLES AND BONNETS *by James 'Thomas' Todd*—Experiences of hard soldiering with the 71st Foot - the Highland Light Infantry - through many battles of the Napoleonic wars including the Peninsular & Waterloo Campaigns

A NORFOLK SOLDIER IN THE FIRST SIKH WAR *by J W Baldwin*—Experiences of a private of H.M. 9th Regiment of Foot in the battles for the Punjab, India 1845-46

A CAVALRY OFFICER DURING THE SEPOY REVOLT *by A.R.D. Mackenzie*—Experiences with the 3rd Bengal Light Cavalry, the Guides and Sikh Irregular Cavalry from the outbreak to Delhi and Lucknow

THE ADVENTURES OF A LIGHT DRAGOON *by George Farmer & G.R. Gleig*—A cavalryman during the Peninsular & Waterloo Campaigns, in captivity & at the siege of Bhurtpore, India

THE COMPLEAT RIFLEMAN HARRIS *by Benjamin Harris as told to & transcribed by Captain Henry Curling*—The adventures of a soldier of the 95th (Rifles) during the Peninsular Campaign of the Napoleonic Wars

THE RED DRAGOON *by W.J. Adams*—With the 7th Dragoon Guards in the Cape of Good Hope against the Boers & the Kaffir tribes during the 'war of the axe' 1843-48

THE LIFE OF THE REAL BRIGADIER GERARD - Volume 1 - THE YOUNG HUSSAR 1782 - 1807 *by Jean-Baptiste De Marbot*—A French Cavalryman Of the Napoleonic Wars at Marengo, Austerlitz, Jena, Eylau & Friedland

THE LIFE OF THE REAL BRIGADIER GERARD Volume 2 IMPERIAL AIDE-DE-CAMP 1807 - 1811 *by Jean-Baptiste De Marbot*—A French Cavalryman of the Napoleonic Wars at Saragossa, Landshut, Eckmuhl, Ratisbon, Aspern-Essling, Wagram, Busaco & Torres Vedras

LEONAUR

ALSO FROM LEONAUR
AVAILABLE IN SOFTCOVER OR HARDCOVER WITH DUST JACKET

THE COMPLEAT RIFLEMAN HARRIS by Benjamin Harris as told to & transcribed by Captain Henry Curling—The adventures of a soldier of the 95th (Rifles) during the Peninsular Campaign of the Napoleonic Wars

WITH WELLINGTON'S LIGHT CAVALRY by William Tomkinson—The Experiences of an officer of the 16th Light Dragoons in the Peninsular and Waterloo campaigns of the Napoleonic Wars.

SERGEANT BOURGOGNE by Adrien Bourgogne—With Napoleon's Imperial Guard in the Russian Campaign and on the Retreat from Moscow 1812 - 13.

SWORDS OF HONOUR by Henry Newbolt & Stanley L. Wood—The Careers of Six Outstanding Officers from the Napoleonic Wars, the Wars for India and the American Civil War, with dozens of illustrations by Stabley L. Wood.

SURTEES OF THE RIFLES by William Surtees—A Soldier of the 95th (Rifles) in the Peninsular campaign of the Napoleonic Wars.

ENSIGN BELL IN THE PENINSULAR WAR by George Bell—The Experiences of a young British Soldier of the 34th Regiment 'The Cumberland Gentlemen' in the Napoleonic wars.

HUSSAR IN WINTER by Alexander Gordon—A British Cavalry Officer during the retreat to Corunna in the Peninsular campaign of the Napoleonic Wars.

NAPOLEONIC WAR STORIES by Sir Arthur Quiller-Couch—Tales of soldiers, spies, battles & sieges from the Peninsular & Waterloo campaingns.

JOURNALS OF ROBERT ROGERS OF THE RANGERS by Robert Rogers—The exploits of Rogers & the Rangers in his own words during 1755-1761 in the French & Indian War.

KERSHAW'S BRIGADE VOLUME 1 by D. Augustus Dickert—Manassas, Seven Pines, Sharpsburg (Antietam), Fredricksburg, Chancellorsville, Gettysburg, Chickamauga, Chattanooga, Fort Sanders & Bean Station..

KERSHAW'S BRIGADE VOLUME 2 by D. Augustus Dickert—At the wilderness, Cold Harbour, Petersburg, The Shenandoah Valley and Cedar Creek.

A TIGER ON HORSEBACK by L. March Phillips—The Experiences of a Trooper & Officer of Rimington's Guides - The Tigers - during the Anglo-Boer war 1899 - 1902.

LEONAUR

ALSO FROM LEONAUR
AVAILABLE IN SOFTCOVER OR HARDCOVER WITH DUST JACKET

SEPOYS, SIEGE & STORM *by Charles John Griffiths*—The Experiences of a young officer of H.M.'s 61st Regiment at Ferozepore, Delhi ridge and at the fall of Delhi during the Indian mutiny 1857.

CAMPAIGNING IN ZULULAND *by W. E. Montague*—Experiences on campaign during the Zulu war of 1879 with the 94th Regiment.

THE STORY OF THE GUIDES *by G. J. Younghusband*—The Exploits of the Soldiers of the famous Indian Army Regiment from the northwest frontier 1847 - 1900..

ZULU: 1879 *by D.C.F. Moodie & the Leonaur Editors*—The Anglo-Zulu War of 1879 from contemporary sources: First Hand Accounts, Interviews, Dispatches, Official Documents & Newspaper Reports.

THE RECOLLECTIONS OF SKINNER OF SKINNER'S HORSE *by James Skinner*—James Skinner and his 'Yellow Boys' Irregular cavalry in the wars of India between the British, Mahratta, Rajput, Mogul, Sikh & Pindarree Forces.

TOMMY ATKINS' WAR STORIES 14 FIRST HAND ACCOUNTS—Fourteen first hand accounts from the ranks of the British Army during Queen Victoria's Empire Original & True Battle Stories Recollections of the Indian Mutiny With the 49th in the Crimea With the Guards in Egypt The Charge of the Six Hundred With Wolseley in Ashanti Alma, Inkermann and Magdala With the Gunners at Tel-el-Kebir Russian Guns and Indian Rebels Rough Work in the Crimea In the Maori Rising Facing the Zulus From Sebastopol to Lucknow Sent to Save Gordon On the March to Chitral Tommy by Rudyard Kipling

CHASSEUR OF 1914 *by Marcel Dupont*—Experiences of the twilight of the French Light Cavalry by a young officer during the early battles of the great war in Europe.

TROOP HORSE & TRENCH *by R. A. Lloyd*—The experiences of a British Lifeguardsman of the household cavalry fighting on the western front during the First World War 1914-18.

THE EAST AFRICAN MOUNTED RIFLES *by C. J. Wilson*—Experiences of the campaign in the East African bush during the First World War.

THE FIGHTING CAMELIERS *by Frank Reid*—The exploits of the Imperial Camel Corps in the desert and Palestine campaigns of the First World War.